PRAISE FOR *HOLDING UP HALF THE SKY*

"Every church should make copies avaiable Graham Joseph Hill's book to everyone who walks in the door. It is peaceful yet firm; biblical without being ornery; theologically sound without become abstractions; pastoral without being condescending; and clear from word one. I endorse and highly recommend Graham Joseph Hill's *Holding Up Half the Sky*."

—SCOT MCKNIGHT,
Professor of New Testament, Northern Seminary

"Graham Joseph Hill can be credited with soundly presenting the case that having women in leadership matters immensely for mission and ministry, not because some radical feminist manifesto said so, but because Scripture and the history of the church proves so. An eminently readable and persuasive case for women to be freed to lead in the local church and in para-church organizations. Books like these often change people's lives!"

—MICHAEL F. BIRD
Academic Dean and Lecturer in Theology, Ridley College

"Graham Joseph Hill offers a helpful study in support of women in ministry which deals both pastorally, practically, and exegetically with the relevant biblical texts and issues in a convincing way. Highly recommended."

—BEN WITHERINGTON III
Amos Professor of New Testament for Doctoral Studies,
Asbury Theological Seminary

"I am grateful for friends like Graham Joseph Hill who fight for women's rightful position in the church. His prophetic voice speaks with distinct truthful clarity about the role of women in the church. *Holding up Half the Sky* examines the historical context and cultural complexities of the early church and the Pauline writings, later advancing towards revealing poignant theological and biblical affirmations of the female presence and their promised roles in the church. Hill's message will shape our understandings of the past and guide our actions in the future."

—GRACE JI-SUN KIM
Associate Professor of Theology, Earlham School of Religion

"Just as Christians today no longer need to argue for the abolition of slavery (despite the existence of many prima facie pro-slavery passages in the Bible), so I hope—with Graham Joseph Hill—that the need to make 'a biblical case for women leading and teaching in the church' will become obsolete. In the interim, books such as these will surely help us in the church get there."

—GRACE YIA-HEI KAO,
Associate Professor of Ethics, Claremont School of Theology; and Co-Director,
Center for Sexuality, Gender, and Religion

"My hope is that this book will reach a new audience who will be assured that women are not secondary in God's plans and that women ministers are not a modern innovation but are present in Scripture. God did not make women only to be assistants of men. God did not intend for women to be restricted to support services within the community of his people. Men and women working in partnership, using their talents and gifts together without artificial restrictions, can only enhance the health and the mission of the church, and this mutuality brings glory to our Lord Jesus."

—MARGARET MOWCZKO,
writer and speaker

"I found it a delight to read Graham Joseph Hill's book, *Holding Up Half the Sky*. It is a wonderful book that clearly and forcefully puts the biblical case for women in leadership without any caveats. It is well-written, well-argued, and well-researched. . . . It has always been true that women hold up half the sky, and this has become undeniably obvious in the last forty years. Appeals to a few texts in the Bible to support the claim that men should be in charge in the church, the home, and in society as well, make no sense in today's world."

—KEVIN GILES
author of *What the Bible Actually Teaches on Women*

"One of the pillars of Missio Alliance's identity and ministry is comprehensive mutuality. We describe this as 'advancing the partnered voice and leadership of women and men among the beautiful diversity of the body of Christ across the lines of race, culture, and theological heritage.' *Holding Up Half the Sky* is nothing short of a biblical manifesto for this conviction. We commend this book as an essential resource for churches on the subject of God's design for female leadership."

—J. R. ROZKO,
National Director, Missio Alliance

"This book belongs on the shelf of anyone exploring the topic of the role of women within the church. Whilst demonstrating respectful and honoring awareness of the range of positions within the church on women in leadership, Graham Joseph Hill offers a robust theological exploration of the topic, looking at the lives of women leaders within the Bible, addressing hotly debated passages in Scripture, and considering the example of Jesus with women. Then, knowing that our beliefs need to be expressed in our practices, Hill brings the conversation into the present day with practical guidance on how to amplify women's voices and honor their gifts and calling."

—Jo Saxton
author of *The Dream of You*

"Graham Joseph Hill's *Holding Up Half the Sky* is a brilliant and compelling summation of the case for women as equal partners with men in the church's ministry. After reading it, it is hard to ignore how unbiblical it is to exclude women from participating in the full authority of the church's offices. The book reads like an emancipation proclamation releasing all God's people, not just men, into the ministry of God's mission in the church."

—David Fitch
Lindner Chair of Evangelical Theology, Northern Seminary

"Graham Joseph Hill has created a compelling and thorough resource! Through deep scriptural engagement, historical insights, and practical actions, *Holding Up Half the Sky* is an essential tool for people passionate to see the full flourishing of women in their context! Hill sheds light on some of the stories of amazing women, who have too often lived in the shadows."

—Nikki Toyama-Szeto
Executive Director, Evangelicals for Social Action, Sider Center

"What Graham Joseph Hill accomplishes in this brief work is remarkable! His careful handling of the Scripture, thorough coverage of contested texts, and compelling case for women as equal partners in all level of church life and leadership, make this book a must read for everyone. Not only does *Holding Up Half the Sky* provide the important biblical case, it also offers practical ways to amplify women's voices and ensure their inclusion and flourishing in the church. I couldn't more highly recommend this book!"

—Lisa Rodriguez-Watson
Leadership Development and Training Director,
Christian Community Development Association

"I am known to highlight favorite sentences in books because they say something that I want to return to, or that I want to share. Graham's book quickly became a colored rainbow of hope. It points to truth, points to a better way for the church, and points to Jesus. I am grateful to Graham for this important book. It will be one that I will be gifting to the next generation to read. Thank you, Graham, for your advocacy."

—JEN BARKER
Founder, Fixing Her Eyes

"Graham Joseph Hill's practice of amplifying voices of women from the global church is rooted in his biblical conviction. This book is a thorough treatment of a biblical case for equality in ministry without ignoring the cultural challenges and opportunities that face us. Graham's excellent intersectionality of social realities with exegetical work makes this a must read."

—SANDRA MARIA VAN OPSTAL
Executive Director, Chasing Justice;
and author of *The Next Worship: Glorifying God in a Diverse World*

"You have in your hands a thorough, well-researched, and compelling biblical and pastoral study, written in accessible language for women and men who are seeking to offer their gifts in the service of Christ. In these pages, Graham Joseph Hill, one of the new generation of scholarly, emerging, global Christian voices, has written a definitive text on gender equality and thus opened a way so that together we may all flourish. I trust it is studied widely and deeply and the possibility it uncovers is able to unfold."

—ANDREW MENZIES
Former Principal, Stirling College—University of Divinity

"Graham Joseph Hill's book *Holding Up Half the Sky* presents a reasoned, logical, and well-argued outline of the debates around women's involvement in the church at various levels of leadership. He outlines the basis for Paul's approach to this issue in detail, centered upon the biblical text and drawing upon some of the best research on the issue from Marg Mowczko, Gail Wallace, Diana Butler Bass, and Julia Baird. This book models a male leader's approach to listening to women, and as such, is a must read for complementarian and egalitarian male leaders alike."

—TANYA RICHES
Senior Lecturer and Masters Program Coordinator, Hillsong College

"This is an outstanding book. Graham Joseph Hill presents a biblically solid and theologically grounded case for why God called men and women to lead and teach in the church."

—SARAH BREUEL
Revive Europe Director and Evangelism Training Coordinator,
International Fellowship of Evangelical Students, Europe

"*Holding up Half the Sky* is a crucial read for those who have a high view on scriptural authority and are concerned for embracing God's mission in this world. In simple language and accessible discussion, Graham Joseph Hill unpacks key biblical passages to demonstrate the central message of ministry by the whole people of God based on gifting and calling. A rich resource for guiding the church to rise above the morass of 'culture wars' to faithful Christian practice in which men and women are equally empowered to lead and serve."

—PERRY SHAW
Professor of Education, Arab Baptist Theological Seminary

"The conversation about men and women in the church has become toxic. Instead of creating a Christlike spirit of peace between men and women, it has contributed to the cultural anxiety. We need imaginative, differentiated voices to draw us out of our anxious striving for a quick fix. Even while providing scriptural guidance, Graham Joseph Hill has found a way to shape a new kind of space, drawing us back into relationship, honesty, and hope. By adding prayers and practices to his teaching, he engages us as whole humans: welcoming our minds, hearts, and spirits back into peace with one another."

—MANDY SMITH
Pastor, University Christian Church; and author of *The Vulnerable Pastor*

"If you are a Christian woman, or know a Christian woman, Graham Joseph Hill's book needs your full attention. This is the book I wish I had written, and the book I wish everyone would read."

—KYLIE MADDOX PIDGEON
Registered Psychologist and Lecturer, St Mark's National Theological Centre,
Charles Sturt University

"I love how honest, fair, and humble this book by Graham Joseph Hill is. It's a simple read and yet it does a solid job of exploring God's word and will. As a woman who is passionate about seeing every person empowered and released to use their gifts for God's kingdom, I highly recommend this book to anyone—wherever you currently land on this topic."

—ESTHER THACKRAY
St. Clair Baptist Church, Sydney, Australia

"What I particularly enjoyed reading this book is Graham Joseph Hill's intent to unpack the issue with grace and clarity. Often the sheer weight of opinion on this topic makes it hard to know where to start. Too often shrouded in the noisy dialogue of culture, complementarianism, and egalitarianism lies the beautiful gospel truth. I recommend this book for anyone seeking an introduction to the biblical case for male and female equality in Christ and ministry."

—PHILIPPA LOWE
Chief Ideas Officer, Incredible Communications

"In stanzas that ring with celebration, examination, confession, and exhortation, this little book invites us to sing an anthem of resounding joy over the gift of mutually submitted, Spirit-empowered service as God's image-bearing people. In it, Graham Joseph Hill helps tune our ears to the Spirit's new creation song, echoed throughout Scripture and the life of the church, in which women and men manifest their priestly calling together for the sake of the world. Hill specifically chorales the ears and voices of brothers to harmonize with those sisters who have, historically and globally, led in singing the gospel of life together in Christ. Thus, we hear the beauty and costly glory of full participation in servantship with Jesus, 'the firstborn among many brothers and sisters.' I recommend this book to churches, friends, and students who want to practice listening for as well as telling the good news of shared ministry under the full sky of God's kingdom."

—CHERITH FEE NORDLING
Associate Professor of Theology, Northern Seminary

"As a female theology student who has felt the call by God to preach, I know I have not been alone in having to justify my position to those who oppose women being called to preach. Graham Joseph Hill has beautifully and gracefully wrestled with these objections by examining complex Bible passages that have led some to their convictions against women preaching. It's a must read for every theological student and curious church member as we learn to work together as brothers and sisters in Christ. We are all called to use our God-given gifts for the advancement of the gospel and to bring glory to our Father. Thank you, Graham, for using your voice to support and advocate for women in ministry."

—MELISSA RAMOO
physiotherapist and theological student

"This compelling book invites the reader to engage in and relate to its every page. The biblical convictions of the author, coupled with his passion and commitment to see women fully involved in the church and ministry, are inspiring. Graham Joseph Hill offers thoughtful and practical insights not only for academics, but also for the average reader. As an Arab woman involved in theological education and church ministry in the Middle East, this book comes as a valuable resource that makes a strong case for the participation of women leaders and teachers in the West, and in no lesser capacity, the East."

—GRACE AL-ZOUGHBI ARTEEN
Head of Biblical Studies Department, Bethlehem Bible College, Palestine

"This book provides a much-needed corrective to the seemingly never-ending egalitarian vs. complementarian and progressivism vs. conservatism debates. Graham Joseph Hill provides straightforward analyses of difficult biblical passages to increase their relevance in twenty-first-century churches. The highlight of this book is fifteen practical steps leaders can take to better incorporate women into church life, so that women can continue to thrive as the 'heartbeat of a living faith.'"

—GINA A. ZURLO
Co-Director, Center for the Study of Global Christianity,
Gordon-Conwell Theological Seminary

"This important book asserts the biblical case for women in leadership and ministry and, in the process, provides evangelical scholars and practitioners with a framework for rigorous scriptural engagement. For all our emphasis on being 'biblical', we can run the risk of approaching the Bible as if we already know what it will say. Graham Joseph Hill approaches the text with great respect, but refuses to allow the traditions of the past to gag the Living God. He reminds us that a scribe discipled in the kingdom will bring forth both old and new treasures from the biblical store."

—GLEN POWELL
Executive Director, Uniting Mission and Education

Holding Up Half the Sky

Holding Up Half the Sky

A Biblical Case for Women Leading
and Teaching in the Church

GRAHAM JOSEPH HILL

Foreword by Grace Ji-Sun Kim
Foreword by Margaret Mowczko
Afterword by Lynn H. Cohick

CASCADE *Books* · Eugene, Oregon

HOLDING UP HALF THE SKY
A Biblical Case for Women Leading and Teaching in the Church

Cascade Books
An Imprint of Wipf and Stock Publishers
199 W. 8th Ave., Suite 3
Eugene, OR 97401

www.wipfandstock.com

PAPERBACK ISBN: 978-1-5326-8611-5
HARDCOVER ISBN: 978-1-5326-8612-2
EBOOK ISBN: 978-1-5326-8613-9

Cataloguing-in-Publication data:

Names: Hill, Graham Joseph, author. | Kim, Grace Ji-Sun, foreword. | Mowczko, Margaret, foreword. | Cohick, Lynn H. afterword.

Title: Holding up half the sky: a biblical case for women leading and teaching in the church. / Graham Joseph Hill; foreword by Grace Ji-Sun Kim; foreword by Margaret Mowczko; afterword by Lynn H. Cohick.

Description: Eugene, OR: Cascade Books, 2019. | Includes bibliographical references.

Identifiers: ISBN 978-1-5326-8611-5 (paperback) | ISBN 978-1-5326-8612-2 (hardcover) | ISBN 978-1-5326-8613-9 (ebook)

Subjects: LCSH: Women clergy—Biblical teaching. | Women in Christianity. | Ordination of women—Christianity. | Women in church work—Biblical teaching.

Classification: BS680.W7 H55 2019 (paperback) | BS680.W7 (ebook)

Manufactured in the U.S.A.   05/27/20

For Grace—
You inspired me to explore these issues and write this book.

Contents

Foreword

GRACE JI-SUN KIM

Women were with Jesus. Mary and Martha, sisters of Lazarus, were Jesus's important friends, and were with Jesus at several events while he was in Jerusalem. Mary stood by Jesus's feet as Martha prepared the meal of the day. Jesus raised Lazarus, their brother, from the dead (John 11:38–41).

The Gospel of Mark says that three women went to the tomb of Jesus to find that the stone had been rolled away. The Gospel of Mark names the women as Mary Magdalene, Mary the mother of James, and Salome (Mark 16:1–8). Once these three women realized that Jesus had risen from the dead, they ran out to tell the disciples of this news. These women were the first evangelists who shared the good news.

In Romans 16, Paul writes about ten female leaders: Phoebe, Priscilla, Mary, Junia, Tryphena, Tryphosa, Persis, Rufus's mother, and Julia. These women were listed for their leadership within the church and their diligent work. These women may have been some of the first to be acknowledged publicly, but women have been an integral part of the church since its birth. Often we forget this truth of Christian history, seldom welcoming women into significant positions, particularly that of leadership positions. We need to remember this part of our past and encourage women to come into leadership in our churches today. It was Martin Luther who wrote "the priesthood of all believers" to emphasize that in congregational life we as individuals are all priests to one another. This belief denotes that women are invariably included as such "priests," and thus we must do the same today.

How did the church come to discourage women from leadership? Historically, Latin patriarchy was mediated and perpetuated through Christianity, and its presence in Christianity has been conserved. Furthermore, parts of the Bible have mediated patriarchal submission and proclaimed God and Christ in patriarchal terms. This patriarchy has defined Christianity and

Christian practices throughout Christian history. The Aristotelian-biblical construct of the inferior human "nature" of slaves and freeborn women has been woven into the fabric of Christian theology.[1] This framework has long prevented women from holding positions of governance in our churches, continuing to keep women subordinated in many Christian denominations. Patriarchy, and the false notion of a nobility of suffering, allows abuse towards women to occur not only in our churches, but within our homes and places of work.[2]

Today, we must work towards repositioning the culture within our churches to be reflexive of its own flaws and combat the established patriarchy that continues to undermine women in worship, government, and business. Men need to be in solidarity with women and work towards breaking down such destructive powers. As men stand in solidarity, we need to engage in conversation that empowers one another.

Rev. Dr. Graham Joseph Hill provides an authentic and a much-demanded male perspective that explores biblical, historical, and doctrinal insights into women and the church. He stands together with women, emphasizing the importance of providing platforms, spaces, and opportunities for women to become strong new leaders in the church and society. This acutely aware and thoughtful book provides readers with the opportunity to reflect on how patriarchy came to be, how it was institutionalized in the church, and how we can ultimately dismantle it.

I am grateful for friends like Graham Joseph Hill who fight for women's rightful position in the church. His prophetic voice speaks with distinct truthful clarity about the role of women in the church. *Holding Up Half the Sky* examines the historical context and cultural complexities of the early church and the Pauline writings, later advancing towards revealing poignant theological and biblical affirmations of the female presence and their promised roles in the church. Hill's message will shape our understandings of the past and guide our actions in the future.

GRACE JI-SUN KIM
Associate Professor of Theology
Earlham School of Religion
Richmond, Indiana

1. Schussler Fiorenza, *But She Said*, 203.
2. Brock and Parker, *Proverbs of Ashes*, 16–18.

Foreword

MARGARET MOWCZKO

Women are involved in all kinds of responsible and demanding work in many countries. Women are doctors, pilots, lawyers, teachers, scientists, journalists, broadcasters, bankers, businesswomen, and they are involved at every level of management. But in many churches, they are excluded from certain ministries and leadership positions. Some Christians believe the Bible teaches that women are prohibited from leadership in the church. Other equally sincere Christians believe that the Bible does not limit capable and called women. Rev. Dr. Graham Joseph Hill discusses this dilemma in his book.

Graham is a husband and father, a lecturer in a theological college in Australia, and someone vitally interested in the global church, and he knows that what we think about the place or the roles of women in the church is not just theoretical. It profoundly affects how both men and women see themselves and each other. It influences relationships between the sexes and how women and girls are treated. It impacts how men and women function in the body of Christ and on the effectiveness of the church's mission. There is a lot at stake here.

In part two of *Holding Up Half the Sky*, Graham examines Bible verses that are often brought up in gender discussions and he provides context to help explain these verses. He notes, for example, that the backdrop of 1 Pet 3:1–6 is "persecution, patriarchy, and unbelieving spouses." Too often, the verses that are used to limit women are not read in context, and so the original intent of the biblical authors and the parameters of their instructions are not factored into interpretation and application. Furthermore, Graham shows that there is a trajectory in Scripture. He writes, "As the pages of the Bible unfold, women's freedoms, dignity, and ministries increase and expand."

I have a keen interest in the biblical arguments that support an egalitarian ethos, but part three of the book is my favorite. In this section, entitled "Embracing the Practices of Biblical Equality," Graham offers encouragement and advice geared at putting equality into practice and making it a reality. Graham's insights here are excellent and inspiring, as is his discussion on the revolutionary nature of biblical "servantship."

Graham has kept his book short and he has kept technical language to a minimum. What is more, it is written especially for all of us deeply involved in local churches.

My hope is that this book will reach a new audience who will be assured that women are not secondary in God's plans and that women ministers are not a modern innovation but are present in Scripture. God did not make women only to be assistants of men. God did not intend for women to be restricted to support services within the community of his people. Men and women working in partnership, using their talents and gifts together without artificial restrictions, can only enhance the health and the mission of the church, and this mutuality brings glory to our Lord Jesus.

MARGARET MOWCZKO
Writer and Speaker
Sydney, Australia
MargMowczko.com

Introduction:
Women Hold Up Half the Sky

By some estimates, over two-thirds of the world's missionaries are women. Fifty-three percent of the world's Christians are women. Christian women are much more likely than Christian men to participate in worship.[1] Most available sources estimate that women do most of the mission in the church worldwide, and probably most of the ministry too.[2] Women pray more than men, and are more likely to say that their faith and religion is important to them. When we consider the ministry women have among children, other women, and men, it's easy to see how women probably do most of the discipling of others in the church worldwide. Mao Zedong once famously said that "women hold up half the sky." Women make up more than half of the church, and most likely do the bulk of the mission, ministry, prayer, worship, and discipleship in the life of the church.

The role of women in Christian ministry has never been free of controversy. Catherine Booth, cofounder of the Salvation Army, had to respond forcefully, for instance, to critics who said that she and other women should not be preaching. In an 1870 pamphlet titled *Female Ministry; or Women's Right to Preach the Gospel*, Catherine Booth wrote: "Making allowance for the novelty of the thing, we cannot discover anything either unnatural or immodest in a Christian woman, becomingly attired, appearing on a platform or in a pulpit. By nature she seems fitted to grace either. God has

---

1. Pew Research Center, "Gender Gap in Religion around the World."

2. Unfortunately, many of these sources rely on historical conjecture. We need further research into the extent to which women do the mission, ministry, and discipling in the church. Thankfully, Dr. Gina Zurlo, Associate Director of the Center for the Study of Global Christianity at Gordon-Conwell, has been awarded a research grant from the Louisville Institute to study women in world Christianity and provide quality data on this matter. "This project seeks to provide the first-ever global quantitative analysis of women in world Christianity to investigate the notion that it is a 'women's movement.'" See the announcement here: https://www.gordonconwell.edu/news/Dr-Gina-Zurlo-Awarded-Research-Grant-To-Study-Women-In-World-Christianity.cfm.

given to woman a graceful form and attitude, winning manners, persuasive speech, and, above all, a finely-toned emotional nature, all of which appear to us eminent natural qualifications for public speaking."[3] Going by the example of Catherine Booth, it seems these qualities also make her suitable to leading and to founding global Christian movements!

Some in the church suggest that women do not make effective leaders. But the latest research into leadership effectiveness, across a wide range of secular, corporate, religious, and not-for-profit organizations, shows the opposite. Not only do women lead effectively, but much of the research indicates that by many measures they lead better than men. In *Scaling Research*, Robert J. Anderson and William A. Adams draw on decades of research into leadership effectiveness among Fortune 500 companies and government agencies. They conclude the following about female leadership, after examining the quality research and data: "To summarize, this data suggests that *women lead more effectively than men*. Since we see a strong positive correlation between Leadership Effectiveness and Creative Competency scores, we conclude that women are more effective because they tend to lead more Creatively and less Reactively. Women leaders are more Creative, more effective, and tend to get better results than men. The predominance of relationship strengths in the Top 10 list suggests that *women* are *more effective because they lead more relationally*. Doing so also requires a high degree of self-awareness and authenticity."[4]

The amount of quality research confirming the same result grows every year. A survey of the leadership effectiveness of 2,780 senior leaders published in the *Harvard Business Review* in 2012 concludes the following:

> At every level, more women were rated by their peers, their bosses, their direct reports, and their other associates as better overall leaders than their male counterparts—and the higher the level, the wider that gap grows . . . Specifically, at all levels, women are rated higher in fully 12 of the 16 competencies that go into outstanding leadership. And two of the traits where women outscored men to the highest degree—taking initiative and driving for results—have long been thought of as particularly male strengths.[5]

---

3. First published under a different title in 1859, the third edition was published in 1870. Booth, *Female Ministry*, ch. 4.

4. Anderson and Adams, *Scaling Leadership*.

5. Zenger and Folkman, "Are Women Better Leaders Than Men?"

This book outlines the biblical vision for women in ministry and leadership. The Bible paints a radical vision of women, empowered and emboldened for full ministry participation in the life of the churches. That's a strong statement! But I'll back it up in the following pages, with careful attention to the biblical witness.

Historically, the way women have been treated by the church and its leaders has been mixed. Following in the way of Jesus, the church has often freed and honored women. In cultures where women were seen as property and sexual objects, the church often treated women as fully human. It's surprising, in one sense, that every woman in Rome didn't convert to Christianity! Christians honored and freed women, and welcomed women into full membership and ministry in the life of the church. The picture hasn't always been so rosy, however. We see many instances in church history where women have been sexually abused, oppressed, and exploited, and prevented from having an equal and honored contribution and voice.

The biblical vision for women, and for their role as teachers, witnesses, disciplers, and leaders, transforms not only personal lives, but also the church and the world. But only the truly biblical vision can do this. This book offers a biblical case for women teaching and leading in the local church and the church worldwide.

"Women hold up half the sky" and they make up more than half of the church. It's due time that the church honored and amplified the voices and gifts of women in the way Jesus intended.

1

Setting the Scene for Biblical Equality

In this book I outline the biblical case for male and female equality in Christ and in ministry. I do not pretend to advance anything original here. And this is not an exhaustive treatment of the texts or the arguments. All I offer is an introductory biblical case for women teaching and leading in the church. I've intentionally kept this book small. Many people have asked me for a summary of the case for biblical equality, so that's what I present here. I recommend a wide range of scholarly books at the end of this book, for those who want to dig deeper in the subject of what the Bible teaches on women in ministry. I hope that people will find this little book to be a useful introductory guide to what the Bible says on this subject.

What follows is my attempt to state my position as honestly and graciously as possible. I am a Bible-believing Christian who believes that God created the genders to be different and complementary. I also believe that the Bible encourages full equality between men and women in Jesus Christ, and full female participation in all forms of ministry and leadership. I seek to do that while honoring those who interpret the Bible differently, and I ask that they do likewise.

Yet I believe that this biblical vision transforms lives, churches, and the world. This is because full gender partnership and equality is God's good and original intention for women and men, and for his world and his church.

I divide this book into three sections. In *section one* I set the scene for biblical equality. In *section two* I outline the biblical vision for women and men in Christ, and present the biblical case for gender equality in ministry. In *section three* I challenge the church to embrace the practical implications of biblical equality.

Before we move into the biblical material it's important to set the scene. This is a heated and complex subject. It can be divisive. Emotions run high. People invest a lot in their convictions and positions on this issue. The subject of women in ministry can serve as a proxy for a wide range of other animosities and anxieties. But this is an important topic for so many reasons. We must deal with it as honestly, fairly, and graciously as possible. And we must seek to be true to the biblical witness. We must put aside false allegations and any desire to "get one up on others." Instead, we should see the challenges and opportunities in this discussion, for church and mission in a changing world.

Romans 12 sets the scene for how we should approach this topic. Paul says these wise words. Let's follow this wisdom in our conversations with and about each other, and in our actions toward each other.

> *Therefore, I urge you, brothers and sisters, in view of God's mercy, to offer your bodies as a living sacrifice, holy and pleasing to God—this is your true and proper worship. Do not conform to the pattern of this world, but be transformed by the renewing of your mind. Then you will be able to test and approve what God's will is—his good, pleasing and perfect will.*
>
> *For by the grace given me I say to every one of you: Do not think of yourself more highly than you ought, but rather think of yourself with sober judgment, in accordance with the faith God has distributed to each of you . . .*
>
> *Love must be sincere. Hate what is evil; cling to what is good. Be devoted to one another in love. Honor one another above yourselves. Never be lacking in zeal, but keep your spiritual fervor, serving the Lord . . . Practice hospitality.*
>
> *Bless those who persecute you; bless and do not curse. Rejoice with those who rejoice; mourn with those who mourn. Live in harmony with one another. Do not be proud, but be willing to associate with people of low position. Do not be conceited.*
>
> *Do not repay anyone evil for evil. Be careful to do what is right in the eyes of everyone . . . Do not be overcome by evil, but overcome evil with good. (Rom 12:1–3, 9–17, 21)*

CAN GODLY MEN BE QUIET?

Before I go any further, I'd like to reflect on the words of Philippa Lowe in her online post, "Can Godly Men Be Quiet?"[1]

Philippa's words challenge and chasten me as I write this book. She says, "The quieter you become, the more you can hear." We men are often too noisy and opinionated to hear. We speak, argue, assert, and posture. We're often so noisy that we can't hear. Our egos and sexisms block our ears and hearts. Philippa says, "So instead, I ask: Godly men, could you be quiet? Because in the quietness you might hear something new. Something Jesus is whispering. That this fuss about women is getting in the way of the Gospel and we need to shush and listen . . . With my hand on my heart for all my Christian brothers who have supported and encouraged me, I have to say . . . Can you please, please, just shush and listen."

Philippa says the greatest gender discrimination she's ever experienced has been in the church and in Christian organizations. My friend Megan Powell du Toit, who is an Australian pastor and academic, puts it this way: "I'm often: ignored, belittled, underestimated, interrupted, patronized, un-cited, my words attributed to men, or given back to me by men as if they originated with them. I find myself often in the awkward position of citing my own credentials and experience. Christian guys . . . please hear me saying this with love and tears . . . I'm sometimes put off contributing on your social media threads because of this."[2]

I'm very conscious of Philippa's and Megan's words as I write this book. Can I be quiet and really listen to what women are saying to me and to the church?

I'm also conscious of the fact that shouting matches between men about what the Bible teaches on women are offensive, useless, and, well, reek of patriarchy, even when some of the interlocutors are advocating for women. "So, instead, can Godly men be quiet in this? Rather than rushing to speak, look at what we are seeing: the diminishment or lack of female voices is having far-reaching impact." My female friends and sisters have their own voice. Will I shush? Will I be quiet and listen?

Being quiet isn't the same as being silent about abuse or oppression, or about equality for women in marriage and ministry. Philippa is right: "There is a difference between quiet and silence. A culture of silence is a

1. Lowe, "Can Godly Men Be Quiet?"
2. Megan Powell du Toit on a post on her Facebook site on February 16, 2019.

breeding ground for abuse. A culture of quiet creates the space for many more to be heard. For the last to be first."

Godly men, it is time to be quiet.

DEALING WITH A HEATED AND COMPLEX SUBJECT

Issues to do with gender and sexuality are hotly debated today. People take and defend positions strongly and with great passion. Opponents level accusations against each other, caricature each other's opinions, and question each other's motives and agendas. People employ rhetorical devices to belittle those who disagree with them and to denigrate the opinions they hold, and to try to convince others to come over to their established position.

We often see this animosity and conflict emerge when Christians discuss the roles women can play in the church. It's a heated topic and accusations fly in all directions.

Those who interpret the Pauline passages in a way that prohibits women from preaching, senior leadership, and public teaching too often suggest that their opponents have a low regard for the authority of the Bible. They suggest that those who encourage women into these ministries have accommodated to contemporary culture, and forsaken biblical faithfulness. One often hears the buzz phrase, "You're just being politically correct" (whatever that means!). Critics of those who support female leadership say that these supporters have interpreted the Bible in a way that fits their hearts and desires, instead of being faithful to a plain reading of the text. These accusations are, of course, hurtful, unfair, and most often untrue. Egalitarian Christians work very hard to be true to the Bible, to honor its authority, and to interpret it accurately. While this may not be true of all egalitarians, I would argue that it is most often the case.

On the other side, those who read Jesus, Paul, and the rest of the Bible in a way that encourages women into full and unrestricted ministry too often suggest that their opponents have a low regard for women. They suggest that those who restrict women have an attachment to patriarchal power, and a desire to oppress, control, and subjugate women. They accuse their opponents of a superficial reading of the Bible, and a hidden agenda that is rooted in power and control, and to the detriment of women and girls. These accusations are, of course, also hurtful, unfair, and most often untrue. Complementarian Christians are usually seeking to be faithful to the Bible and its instructions, and they have a high regard for women. They believe that following the Bible's instructions carefully will be to the benefit of all in the church: women and men. While this may not be true of all complementarians, again I would assert that it is most often the case.

We must seek after light and truth in the midst of all this conflict and heat.

Egalitarian evangelicals and complementarian evangelicals are both seeking to be faithful to the Bible and to the gospel. They both care about the well-being of the whole church and advancement of the gospel. This is also very often the case, of course, among those who debate these issues but do not self-identify with the term "evangelical."

The difficulty we face is that we are dealing with a heated and complex issue. The theological, biblical, historical, cultural, gender, and literary contexts are many and overlapping. If it wasn't difficult interpreting these biblical texts, we wouldn't have so many Bible-believing Christians and scholars debating them, over so many centuries.

In addition to the interpretive complexities we have the anxiety created by the culture wars. Those who want to maintain what they consider to be traditional and conservative values and gender roles struggle with those who hold a more progressive and socially liberal view of the world. As the church in the West declines many Christians get caught up in these culture wars, viewing their conservative or progressive positions as hills to die on.

The role of women in ministry then becomes a proxy for these struggles. As the church feels under threat from the culture, and is faced with its own failures and decline, it is very tempting to choose one or two issues to take a stand on as representations of our "conservativism" or "progressivism." The evangelical response to women's liberation and feminism has been no exception.

So, what do we do with all that? I'm not going to pretend to have all the answers. But I think we need to seek to be faithful interpreters of the Bible, while honoring those who come to a different conclusion than ours.

This means choosing not to caricature others or denigrate their motives or agendas. It means seeking peace and mutual respect, and staying open to conversations where we learn from each other. And it means giving our congregations, young people, and students the chance to wrestle with the various positions on women in ministry, so that they might arrive at their own conclusions, even if these differ from ours. After all, the Bible commends the Berean Jews for their noble character. Why? "They received the message with great eagerness and examined the Scriptures every day to see if what Paul said was true" (Acts 17:11).

We also need to own our anxieties and insecurities in the face of a changing culture. We must stay open to conversation, friendship, and the latest biblical scholarship. And we must acknowledge the complexities involved in interpreting these Bible passages well.

All of that takes grace and maturity. It means imitating Christ. "In humility value others above yourselves, not looking to your own interests but each of you to the interests of the others" (Phil 2:1–11).

ACKNOWLEDGING THE IMPORTANCE OF THE DISCUSSION

I'll be honest. I used to find this conversation irritating and wearying. I live in Sydney, Australia; a heartland of evangelical conservatism. Some of our Sydney churches never stop talking about gender roles and prohibitions on women in ministry. It can get tiring. But, over the last few decades the debates here in Sydney have become more and more heated. The old suspicions and animosities have only deepened. So, it's important to investigate these biblical passages afresh, in a spirit of openness and dialogue, acknowledging the importance of the issue.

The discussion about the role of women in leadership is important for a number of reasons. Here I offer a few.

Firstly, the matter of biblical truth is at stake. This is no trivial matter. Are we being true to the Bible and the gospel message? Are we being faithful to the witness of Jesus and the early church? Are we interpreting to suit our own agendas and interests, or reading faithfully and humbly, and seeking the truth? If we are reading the Bible faithfully it will often expose our desires, contradict our opinions, reveal our sin and weakness, and reshape our way of seeing the world. Whether our interpretation of the Bible contradicts or affirms our culture isn't important. Contradicting the culture is no sign of biblical faithfulness. What matters is the approval of God and "correctly handling the word of truth" (1 Tim 2:15).

Biblical truth and gospel faithfulness are more important than whether we agree with or disagree with our culture. We must relinquish our posturing and point scoring and seek God's truth in a spirit of prayer and humility.

Secondly, females make up more than 50 percent of the global church. We had better be sure we are interpreting the Bible accurately on this matter, when it affects more than half of all believers. Before I prohibit more than half the church from public teaching and preaching or from senior leadership, I had better be sure I am interpreting these Bible texts correctly. Before I encourage such a large group of believers into such ministries, I had better do the same. The implications if we get this wrong are enormous; for the well-being of believers, the health of our churches, and the vitality of our witness.

Thirdly, women and girls have, historically, been oppressed and taken advantage of in many cultures. Jesus honored women, and freed them from shame, invisibility, and indignity. His actions were in unambiguous contrast to his society, and the early church sought to honor women in the imitation of their Lord. As I said earlier, it's surprising, in one sense, that every woman in the Roman Empire didn't convert to Christianity and the freedom and honor it offered women and their children. Sadly, throughout the ages, and across a multitude of cultures and contexts, the church hasn't always treated women this way. As our culture rightly reminds us—women and girls have often been abused and exploited by our churches and their leaders. This is not an argument for a complementarian or egalitarian position, as I believe we need to take the biblical texts on their own merit. But it must make us pause to ensure that whatever position we take truly results in all people being dignified, honored, freed, and affirmed—women, children, and men alike.

For these and many other reasons, the matter of women teaching and leading in the church is important today. We must give it careful and mature biblical, historical, and theological treatment.

ADDRESSING THE SPIRITUAL
OPPORTUNITIES AND CHALLENGES

We face many challenges as we enter this discussion and wrestle with the implications of our convictions.

It's challenging for us to see where our view on women in ministry sits within our broader denominational tradition and theological system. How is our view on women in ministry informed and shaped by that system and church culture? Is it coincidental that Calvinists tend to be some form of complementarian? Or that egalitarians are found more in Quakers, United Methodist Churches, The Presbyterian Church (USA), Northern Baptists, the Wesleyan Church, and some Pentecostal churches? Is that because we are consistent in the way we interpret and read the Bible? Or is it because we've bought a whole theological worldview, completely and entirely, and without question? If we really examined the Bible for ourselves would we end up in the same position on most issues as our pastor, our denomination, or our preferred theological position? I highly doubt it. Coming to independently owned convictions is hard work. But it's the work of Christian maturity and discipleship.

The other challenge is refusing to adopt an entirely "conservative" or "progressive" stance. (And refusing to caricature someone else that way.) A mature set of convictions may mean that I am progressive on issues of justice, but conservative on gender roles. Or I may be progressive on gender roles, but conservative on abortion. We need to develop a consistent approach to interpreting the Bible (a biblical hermeneutic) and then apply it faithfully in each instance.

Let me offer one final challenge: that of intellectual and spiritual humility and courage. Once we adopt a position, it's easy for pride and ego to take over. We've staked our position and we're not budging. But if our desire is to be true to the Bible's teaching, and to be faithful to Jesus and his gospel, then we must be willing to change. Change is difficult. It can be painful. It takes courage. And if our new view is in contrast to the position of those around us (and especially our church leaders), then change can come at a high personal price. But change is part of discipleship and spiritual growth. And it requires intellectual and spiritual depth and humility. Jesus showed us in his own life that humility and self-sacrifice is painful and costly, and it takes courage and selflessness.

SUMMARIZING THE COMPLEMENTARIAN AND EGALITARIAN POSITIONS

Before we go any further, it is worth summarizing what we mean by the complementarian and egalitarian positions.

In *Bourgeois Babes, Bossy Wives, and Bobby Haircuts*, Michael Bird offers a useful account of the views of each group.[3] He rightly notes that there are probably (at least) four positions: Christian Feminism, Evangelical Egalitarianism, Moderate Complementarianism, and Hierarchical Complementarianism. Here's how Bird characterizes these four positions:

Christian feminists deny gender differences, and see women as an oppressed group. Women must be liberated from male domination, including the patriarchal stories and themes in the Bible.

3. Bird, *Bourgeois Babes, Bossy Wives, and Bobby Haircuts*, 16–18.

Evangelical egalitarians advocate for equality between men and women in the home and the church. Women can hold any office in the church, and perform any ministry, based on their gifts and callings, not on their gender. The Pauline texts that seem to restrict women's ministries are not universal prohibitions—they are specific instructions for particular contexts.

Moderate complementarians encourage women to teach women and children, but prohibit them from serving in church offices such as senior pastor or teaching elder. Women can offer a message to a mixed-gender congregation as long as they are under the oversight of a male pastor or elder.

Hierarchical complementarians restrict women's ministries to leadership among children and other women. Women may not hold any leadership office or function in the church where they might exercise authority over men.

Of course, the terms "complementarian" and "egalitarian" are recent inventions, and not always helpful. Kevin Giles offers a useful background to the origin and development of these terms.[4] The labels can be misleading, and they come with a lot of baggage. Nonetheless, we must understand what these terms signify.

DOING AWAY WITH FALSE ALLEGATIONS

Why would Christians seek to restrict the ministries women can do in the church? Klyne Snodgrass proposes the following: "The early church may well have thought the question strange. Only three reasons exist to restrict the ministry of women: the tradition of patriarchy, the influence of two NT texts (1 Cor 14:33–38 and 1 Tim 2:9–15), and an unjust and inflated view of church office."[5]

Snodgrass then says that we need to deal with three misconceptions, as we arrive at a biblical case for the unrestricted ministry of women. I quote these at length, because they need to be dealt with early on in the discussion.

I make three assertions now, and then deal with the misconceptions that require such assertions be made.

1. *Support for women in ministry is* not *a result of feminism and an assault on traditional values.*

4. Giles, *What the Bible Actually Teaches on Women*, 45.
5. Snodgrass, "Case for the Unrestricted Ministry of Women," 1–2.

9

The first [misconception] views the concern for women in ministry as a result of feminism and an assault on traditional values. The issue of women in ministry has *not* emerged merely because of feminism, although feminism and other cultural factors have certainly heightened the discussion . . . The traditional view is not necessarily Christian; it is present in virtually every culture and has led to patriarchy, views of the inferiority of women, abuse, and limitation of women's roles. If we think we are preserving some greater spiritual practice by limiting women, why is it that Christian practices in traditional churches and most other churches relating to sexuality, divorce, abuse, etc. do not differ from practices in the broader secular society, at least in the U.S. and Europe? The NT challenges the cultural deviations of both past and present. Christianity needs to stand for and embody a rejection of the failures of society. It is clear that women have a role, a responsibility, and gifts to help the church communicate and live its message. Without the exercise of their gifts the church is diminished.[6]

I've lost track of the amount of times I've heard complementarians say supporting women in ministry is a "feminist agenda" driven by the concerns and values of a "post-gender Western culture." They claim that the goal is to empower women to pursue their own version of "patriarchal, worldly power" by usurping men. Those charges are completely untrue, and amount to false accusations. The true goal of those supporting women in ministry is to move beyond the values of traditional or progressive cultures, and, instead, be true to what the Bible teaches. What do we learn from the way Jesus treated women? What does the Bible really teach on women, and on their participation in preaching, ministry, and mission?

2.   *Support for women in ministry is* not *a result of a low view of the authority of the Bible.*

The second misconception is that a decision on this issue depends on whether one is theologically liberal or conservative generally or whether one believes fully in the authority of Scripture. Neither is true . . . Regarding Scripture, people with equally high views of Scripture are on both sides of the debate. Indeed, many of us argue for the full ministry of women because Scripture pushes us to that conclusion.

Another common false accusation is that people who support women in ministry are theologically liberal or have abandoned a high view of the

6. Snodgrass, "Case for the Unrestricted Ministry of Women," 1.

authority of Scripture. Again, this is totally untrue. I've seen some complementarians even say that they embrace a positive "literal reading of the Bible" while egalitarians are merely offering "interpretations." This is misleading rhetoric, and quite dishonest. In my experience, most evangelicals and Bible-believing Christians of other traditions (of both complementarian and egalitarian persuasions) have a very high view of the authority of the Bible. Let's honor each other, and do away with false and misleading accusations. The goals we all share are: (1) to love the Lord our God with all our heart and soul and mind and strength; (2) to love our neighbor as ourselves; (3) to rightly interpret and teach the truth of the gospel and the words of the Bible; (4) to preach the gospel of Jesus Christ, that all might be saved; (5) and to have our hearts and lives and churches and world changed as a result.

3. *Support for women in ministry is not linked with a support for LGBTI issues.*

> A third misconception is that acceptance of women in ministry is a step towards acceptance of the legitimacy of homosexual practice. The fear of homosexuality is a motivating factor for some arguing against the unlimited ministry of women, but there is no necessary relation between the two issues and significant hermeneutical differences in the discussion of the pertinent biblical texts on these two subjects.

There is no link between what a person believes about women in ministry and what they believe about LGBTI issues. Again, to suggest that a link exists is devious and quite dishonest.

It is important to deal with those three common misconceptions early in this book, since they come up in complementarian sermons, books, and blogs way too often.

HONORING CURRENT AND HISTORICAL WOMEN LEADERS IN THE CHURCH

Male Christian leaders often get recognized and applauded. But what about their female contemporaries? We should honor women in leadership and ministry more often; both current and historical female leaders.

ıen are, and always have been, the heartbeat of living faith.[7] Di-
ır Bass used that phrase in a recent interview, and I really love it.
are at the center of Christian faith, discipleship, worship, ministry,
,y, community, and mission. Stephen Bevans describes how the "average Christian" today is female, black, and lives in a Brazilian favela or an
African village.[8] Globally, Christian women are more spiritually active than
men, and also more persecuted.

Diana Butler Bass recently wrote the following:

> I hope that we will finally get beyond the idea of "Christian women
> leaders" being some special subset of Christian community. Wom-
> en are the majority of Christians around the world—we are the
> heartbeat of living faith. The media spends too much time covering
> male leaders—and then a small subset of authoritarian conservative
> men—as if they are the voice of the church. They are not. Women
> are. All the women. The women who preach, the women who write
> theology, the women who pray, the women who serve, those who
> hold the hand of the dying. Those who care for children, those who
> feed the hungry, those who embrace the poor and visit prisoners.
> Those who weep and mourn for the pain they've suffered. Those
> who find that God's love is more beautiful and trustworthy than
> those who abused them. That's the church—a church that knows
> no facile forgiveness or partisan spin. But the church that under-
> stands grace, peacemaking, and mercy. And that church is rarely
> heard in public because it is too busy living its faith.[9]

Women are, and always have been, the heartbeat of living faith.

Reta Halteman Finger has helped me see that nothing shaped the theology, community, and mission of the early church more than the people
at its heart.[10] For the early church, these people were women, the poor, the
sick, the outcast, the powerless, and the marginalized. These groups formed
the nucleus of the ancient church. They understood themselves as following
after the example and mission of Christ.

Men had an important role to play, of course. Men have an important
role to play in the church today, as women and men and children—of all

7. I first published some of these thoughts in a blog post called "Women are the
Heartbeat of Living Faith."

8. Bevans et al., "Missiology after Bosch," 69.

9. Diana Butler Bass in an interview with Carol Kuruvilla for the Huffington Post,
October 15, 2016.

10. Finger, *Of Widows and Meals.*

ethnicities and languages and income and social classes—come together as a new family and a new humanity in Christ. But for thousands of years, men have had all the power, recognition, opportunities, and voice. We've neglected the people who are the heartbeat of living faith.

Women, the poor, the sick, the outcast, the powerless, and the marginalized weren't just a part of the early church community. And they didn't just heavily influence the early church community. They were at the heart of the community. Women, the poor, and the socially marginalized shaped the theology, fellowship, service, discipleship, and mission of the early church, in immense and incalculable ways.

Jesus reinvents the family. He creates an intentional community. The early church was a community of open homes, economic sharing, communal meals, and spiritual family. Within this extended family, people met each other's economic and social needs. These churches abolished acquisition of wealth and honor by patronage. They met daily in homes and around meals. They prized loyalty, love, faith, welcome, hospitality, hope, diversity, equality, truth telling, and grace.

And Jesus chose women to be at the heart of this community. Their love and hospitality and passion shaped the early church.

The same is true today, all over the globe. Women are the heartbeat of living faith. They are the voice and hands and heart of the church.

Jesus reimagines family and household and male/female relations. This has profound implications for the church. It has massive consequences for our theologies, gender relations, communal sharing, and mission in the world. It allows women all over the church to rise up, use their gifts, and show leadership.

Phoebe, for instance, was a highly regarded woman in the church of Cenchreae, a deacon, and a respected patron. The hospitable women of Acts 2, 4, and 6 are sometimes hidden in the text. But they're the backbone of the church and its mission. These women showed that faith isn't merely a private or religious affair. These women's actions reveal the power of the gospel to shape the social, political, sexual, economic, ethical, and other aspects of our lives.

Women were crucial to shaping the early church, and turning it into a family on mission. And women continue to do the same today.

It shouldn't surprise us that women are the heartbeat of living faith. As Dorothy Sayers once observed, women have met a Man like no other. And they choose to follow him, and shape a church that reflects his welcome, diversity, equality, and kinship.[11]

Jesus honored and welcomed women. He invited them to join with him in forming a new spiritual family. He invited them to carry his message and vision, embodying his love and welcome and peacemaking. He invited them to join fully with him in his mission. And, so, in the ancient and modern church, locally and globally, women are the heartbeat of living faith.

There are many examples of current and historical women Christian leaders we can honor. Why don't we celebrate them more? Their gifts, passions, and ministries can inspire women and men alike.

Here are a few examples of Christian women leaders who inspire me:

Leoncia Rosado Rosseau, also known as Mama Leo, founded the Iglesia Cristiana Damascus and envisioned a ministry among drug addicts that for years has been an integral attempt to do mission. Rosado Rosseau was a groundbreaking Puerto Rican evangelist who worked in drug rehabilitation and established the Damascus Christian Church. She championed women's rights and battled sexism in ministry and society. She helped change so many lives through her care, passion, and pioneering and prophetic spirit. Many addicts were transformed by Rosado Rosseau's ministry and pastoral care, and she served as a role model for a generation of young women in Christian ministry.

Elin Sarkissian is writing her second Farsi-language worship album. Her music and interviews have been broadcast internationally and have brought God's message of hope into Iran and many countries around the world.

MaryKate Morse is Leadership Professor and lead mentor at Portland Seminary for their Doctor of Ministry program in Leadership and Spiritual Formation. She is a Friends Minister, has planted two churches, was a missionary, and understands the challenges of being a woman leader in the church. She has authored two books and is involved with *Missio Alliance* and travels internationally speaking on leadership, the church, and spiritual formation. She draws insightfully on issues in culture and society. She is also a spiritual director. She has accomplished a lot, but it is her story and what she committed to being as a spiritual leader that inspires countless others.

Elaine McCormack was one of the first women to graduate from the Baptist Theological College in NSW/ACT, Australia, in the 1960s. She worked incredibly hard as a single woman caring for three congregations

11. Sayers, *Are Women Human?*, 69.

on the Northern Rivers of New South Wales. It's women like Elaine who paved the way for future generations of Australian female Christian pastors.

Catherine Booth founded the Salvation Army with her husband William. Catherine's ministry was extraordinary. She visited and cared for people in the slums, and provided food and clothing for children and families in need. She established shelters for homeless people, and helped the Salvation Army set up a factory for low-paid workers, with better pay and conditions. She campaigned against the use of cancer-causing chemicals, and against what amounted to modern-day slavery. She helped people find employment, and worked to better the lives of drug addicts and alcoholics. Catherine sought freedom and dignity for prostitutes, and campaigned against the abuse of women and children. She spoke up for gender equality, and advocated for the right for women to preach and teach. Catherine was a revivalist, social reformer, cofounder of a radical Christian movement, political activist, gospel preacher, and champion of women's rights.

Melba Padilla Maggay lives in the Philippines. She's a writer, theologian, political activist, sociologist, and highly respected Christian leader. She's the founder and director of the Institute for Studies in Asian Church and Culture (ISACC), based in Quezon City in the Philippines. Melba gained international prominence and acclaim through her writings, through her social and political leadership, and through her work to transform broken communities. She was instrumental in organizing the Protestant presence at the EDSA barricades during the February People Power Uprising in the Philippines in 1986. Melba founded ISACC, which has a vision "to see the gospel of Christ so rooted in Asian cultures that they are engaged by its values and empowered to become societies of justice and righteousness."[12]

Tara Beth Leach is the Senior Pastor at First Church of the Nazarene of Pasadena ("PazNaz") in Southern California. She is a regular writer for *Missio Alliance* and has contributed to other publications such as *Christianity Today, Christian Week,* and *The Jesus Creed.* Her book *Emboldened: A Vision for Empowering Women in Ministry* is encouraging and inspiring a new generation of female and male Christian leaders.

Ruth Padilla DeBorst is the provost of the Centro de Estudios Teológicos Interdisciplinarios. Ruth is a leading voice globally on integral and urban mission. She's involved in leadership with the Latin American Theological Fellowship, and also with Micah Global and INFEMIT (The International Fellowship for Mission as Transformation). Ruth and her

12. http://isaccnet.weebly.com/about-us.html.

family have been engaged in integral mission, leadership development, and theological education in Latin America (and globally) for many years. Ruth lives in Costa Rica where she shares parenting of their blended, multicultural family with her husband, James Padilla DeBorst, and community life with the members of Casa Adobe. Ruth's perspectives on integral mission, holistic theological education, service with and among the poor, and cultivating transformative local communities, are prophetic.

Julia Baird is both an outstanding scholar and public intellectual, who has made a sustained and distinguished contribution to the wider community in the areas of justice, equality, and religion. Julia is a dedicated Christian who has made a significant and ongoing contribution to the Australian and international community in the area of society and religion. She is well known in Australia as a journalist, broadcaster, and author, and is host of *The Drum* on ABC TV. Julia has recently risen to further national prominence with her extensive investigation of domestic abuse in Christian and pastoral families. In mid-2017, she released her findings on Australian television current affairs program the *ABC 7.30 Report*, and showed how many Christian women endure domestic abuse. Her research involved interviewing dozens of survivors of domestic abuse, as well as church psychologists, denominational leaders, and clergy. Her research also investigated domestic violence and Islam (even though her investigation into violence within Christianity has received the most attention). Julia says that when women are heard, change will happen.

Felicity Hill is one of the most gifted Christian leaders I have ever met. She oversees a multimillion-dollar aged-care facility in Sydney with enormous skill and devotion. She treats the many hundreds of staff, residents, and families with compassion, dignity, and care, and is widely recognized as an extraordinarily gifted Christian leader and manager. Felicity is passionate about people and seeing them succeed and ensuring quality care and compassion is shown to all.

Jo Saxton is an author, speaker, leadership coach, visionary, and entrepreneur, who empowers women, challenges societal stereotypes, and helps people discover who they truly are, by seeing themselves the way God sees them. Born to Nigerian parents and raised in London, Jo brings a multicultural and international perspective to leadership. She has served on staff in multiple churches in the United Kingdom and the United States, and as the board chair of a nonprofit organization. Today Jo is the founder of the *Ezer Collective*, an initiative that invests in and equips women leaders. She is also an executive producer and cohost of the popular podcast *Lead Stories: Tales of Leadership in Life* with Steph O'Brien.

Grace Ji-Sun Kim is a remarkable Korean-American scholar who has written or edited sixteen books and over seventy articles and book chapters. Her passion for Jesus and his people is truly inspiring.

As we look across the current and historical church, we see millions of women in leadership and ministry. Sometimes they are in public and visible roles, but often they go unnoticed, quietly serving God's people and working to make the world a better place. They come from every culture, language, theological tradition, ethnicity, age, era, and continent. Women have always made up more than half of the church, so it shouldn't surprise us that women do so much ministry in the church and the world.

God's people must get much better at acknowledging and honoring those women who are our current and historical leaders.

2

Presenting the Scriptural Case
for Biblical Equality

Let's turn now to the biblical case for women in ministry, starting with the example set by our Lord Jesus Christ. From there we move to the background for Paul's teaching on women and men. We look at how women served in the early churches, and the leadership roles they played in the Old and New Testaments. We also examine the contentious biblical passages and ask two things: First, what do they tell us about women and men in Christ? Second, what do we do with them today?

IMITATING THE WAY JESUS HONORED WOMEN—
JOHN 4, LUKE 10 AND 24, AND MARK 14

Religions can be oppressive or freeing. We see this in Christianity as much as any other religion. Over and over again I've heard Christian women express frustrations about the way Christian theology is used to severely limit women's rights, independence, leadership, and contributions. They feel ignored by their churches and leaders. They feel their contributions and gifts are devalued. They feel their rights are limited. They feel their voices are silenced. They feel they are called to lead but are unable to do so. They find many examples of female leaders across the history of their Christian faith and ask why they shouldn't be able to similarly lead? Is this the result of Christian doctrine and Scriptures? Or is something else going on among Christian communities that is limiting female leadership?

Religion can damage, oppress, silence, and ignore women. But faith communities can also honor, elevate, value, celebrate, listen to, and respect women.

As Christians, we need "women at the table" in our churches and organizations. Otherwise, we lose so much, make women feel insignificant and valueless, and encourage women to question or abandon their faith. Why are religious institutions so dominated by men, and especially by their egos and insecurities? We can't build strong, deep, diverse, Spirit-led communities without women at the table.

Religions have an important role to play in amplifying the voices of women. For too long, our Western cultures have focused on the role of economic and political powers to liberate women. But given the importance of religion in so many people's lives, we'll never see women fully honored and released until we address the role that religion has to play in magnifying the voices and valuing the contributions of women. How can women have rights, or feel welcomed and honored and embraced, without a seat at the religious table?

We need an alternative narrative; one that welcomes women at the table, just as Jesus did. These women help to challenge our distorted and dysfunctional gendered roles, religious systems, and discriminatory messaging.

Jesus honored women and welcomed them at the table. Dorothy Sayers once observed that when women met Jesus, they met a Man like no other. And they chose to follow him, and shaped a church that reflected his welcome, hospitality, love, and equality. She writes,

> Perhaps it is no wonder that the women were first at the Cradle and last at the Cross. They had never known a man like this Man— there never has been such another. A prophet and teacher who never nagged at them, never flattered or coaxed or patronized; who never made arch jokes about them, never treated them either as "The women, God help us!" or "The ladies, God bless them!"; who rebuked without querulousness and praised without condescension; who took their questions and arguments seriously; who never mapped out their sphere for them, never urged them to be feminine or jeered at them for being female; who had no axe to grind and no uneasy male dignity to defend; who took them as he found them and was completely unself-conscious.[1]

1. Sayers, *Are Women Human?*, 68–69.

Jesus honored and welcomed women. He invited them to join with him in forming a new spiritual family. He invited them to carry his message and vision, embodying his love and welcome and peacemaking. He invited them to join with him in his mission. He honored and welcomed women fully.

We can't deny that Jesus chose twelve male disciples. As N. T. Wright explains, there were practical and cultural reasons why this was so. There were also symbolic reasons: the twelve apostles symbolized the male heads of the old tribes of Israel. But women were intimately involved in his ministry, and he honored them in a way that contrasted with the existing culture and religious establishment.

N. T. Wright highlights the story of Mary and Martha in Luke 10 as one striking example. Often when we hear this story in a sermon, the focus is on Mary's devotion. But that's not the most remarkable thing about this story. Wright points out that first-century readers, and many readers in modern Middle Eastern cultures, would have marveled "at the fact that Mary was sitting at Jesus's feet *within the male part of the house* rather than being kept in the back rooms with the other women."[2]

This was a scandalous, countercultural action. It broke all the basic social conventions. Jesus welcomed her among the men and declared that she has every right to be there. No wonder Martha was agitated! N. T. Wright makes the point that "sitting at the teacher's feet" is no passive activity. Think of Paul sitting at Gamaliel's feet. The aim of students is to actively absorb the teaching of the master, in order to become teachers themselves. The first-century reader would not have missed this point! N. T. Wright concludes, "That, no doubt, is part at least of the reason why we find so many women in positions of leadership, initiative and responsibility in the early church; I used to think Romans 16 was the most boring chapter in the letter, and now, as I study the names and think about them, I am struck by how powerfully they indicate the way in which the teaching both of Jesus and of Paul was being worked out in practice."[3]

In *What the Bible Actually Teaches on Women*, Kevin Giles has a brilliant chapter called "Jesus, The Best Friend Women Have Ever Had."[4] He rightly says that we should not set Paul over against the example and teaching of Jesus. We are disciples of Jesus, after all. He is our Lord and Savior, and our teacher and example. I encourage you to read Giles's chapter.

2. Wright, "Women's Service in the Church."
3. Wright, "Women's Service in the Church."
4. Giles, *What the Bible Actually Teaches on Women*, ch. 5.

Here are just a few of Kevin Giles's observations about the way Jesus treated women. Jesus had female disciples. In fact, they were intimately involved in his life and ministry. Jesus invited both women and men to follow him, without distinction (Mark 8:34). The way Jesus related to women, especially given the cultural context, was astonishing. The examples are numerous. In first-century Judaism, men did not speak with women in public who were not their wives—yet Jesus both spoke with women and touched them. Astonishing. No wonder so many women followed him.

Kevin Giles notes four powerful examples.

First, in John 4 we have the story of Jesus's encounter with the woman at the well. Jesus has a theological conversation with her, then commands her to go back to her village to preach and evangelize.

Second, in Luke 10 we have the story of Mary and Martha, where Jesus breaks all social conventions to welcome Mary among the men and to allow her to "sit at his feet." As I mentioned, this is an active "sitting" with the intention of teaching the words and message of the teacher. One sits at the feet of the teacher in order to become a teacher. Talk about a dramatic challenge to the prevailing limitations on women, and to the norms of the culture!

Third, in Mark 14 we have the story of Jesus's anointing by a woman. Don't miss the fact that she was assuming a prophetic role, reserved, up to that point, for men. She is publicly declaring that Jesus is the Messiah. Jesus welcomes her ministry—like an Old Testament prophet she anointed the head of the King.

Fourth, the risen Jesus appears first to women (Matt 28:1–10; Mark 16:1–8; Luke 24:1–12; John 20:1–18). I love this part of the gospel! The risen Jesus chooses to appear first to the women and gives them an apostolic mission: "Go and tell the other disciples that Jesus is risen!" Thomas Aquinas called these women the "apostles to the twelve apostles." The male disciples were frightened and had given up hope. The female disciples continued watching and hoping and waiting on their Lord. Jesus appears to them and sends them to declare the gospel to the apostles. "He is risen as he said he would!" These women become "apostles to the twelve apostles." Such a powerful and important story! It says much about the heart of Jesus and the way that he honors women and releases them to full and equal contribution and witness. Andreas and Margaret Kostenberger helpfully acknowledge the following: "By appearing first to a woman, the risen Jesus implicitly challenged the patriarchal culture of his day that did not consider women as viable legal witnesses."[5] Yes! That's the story of the way Jesus treats and honors women.[6]

There are many other examples, but when we start looking at these stories we see why the early church so honored and amplified the voices and ministries of women. They followed after the example set by their Lord.

Tragically, the church has too often forgotten the example set by Jesus Christ. Jesus honored women in ways that contrasted with the prevailing culture. But, too often, the misogyny and oppression and abuse of women in the church has mirrored the culture.

Dorothy Sayers describes how the women who met Jesus were astonished by his respect for them, and his elevation of their contribution and dignity. But she ends on a sad note:

> There is no act, no sermon, no parable in the whole Gospel that borrows its pungency from female perversity; nobody could possibly guess from the words and deeds of Jesus that there was anything "funny" about women's nature. But we might easily deduce it from His contemporaries, and from His prophets before Him, and from His Church today. Women are not human; nobody shall persuade that they are human; let them say what they like, we will not believe it, though One rose from the dead.[7]

It is time for the church to affirm—as their Lord does—the full humanity and contribution and gifts of women.

EXAMINING A THEOLOGY OF GENESIS AND THE CREATION ORDER—GENESIS 1–3

Genesis 1–3 are crucial passages for our understanding of what it means to be men and women, and how we should relate to each other. The Old Testament scholar Richard Hess says, "The account of creation, the garden of Eden and the fall in Genesis 1–3 may contain more doctrinal teaching concerning the nature of humanity as male and female, as well as the state of our fallen world, than any other text in the Bible."[8]

---

5. Köstenberger and Köstenberger, *God's Design for Man and Woman*, 107.

6. Giles, *What the Bible Actually Teaches on Women*, 83–84.

7. Sayers, *Are Women Human?*, 69.

8. Pierce et al., *Discovering Biblical Equality*, 79.

Some complementarians use Genesis to claim that gender roles are part of the "created order." But a closer examination of Genesis 1–3 doesn't support that claim. In fact, the *only* suggestion of an unequal relationship occurs *after* the fall, and as a negative consequence of fallenness and sinfulness.

In Genesis 1–3, we see that men and women are equally created in God's image (Gen 1:27). One was created before the other sequentially, but that in no way implies hierarchy. In fact, the emphasis of this passage is on intimacy, unity, companionship, and love (Gen 2:18–25). God gives them equal domination over creation, to care for creation together as co-stewards and equal partners (Gen 1:28). The woman is created as a "helper" and partner, but there is nothing in this passage to suggest that they are not equal partners, serving together equally (Gen 2:20–24). There is also nothing in this passage to suggest that the woman is subordinate to the man, or that they have differentiated "roles." It is only after the fall that we see a suggestion of conflict and power emerge, as one desires to rule over the other, and as animosities and power plays begin to arise (Gen 3:16). But we are the people of *the new creation* not the people of the fall!

Richard Hess writes of Genesis 1–3: "There is neither explicit nor implicit mention of authority or leadership roles of the man over the woman, except as the sad result of their sin in the Fall and their ensuing judgments. Even then, such hierarchy is not presented as an ideal, but rather as a reality of human history like that of the weeds that spring form the earth. The resolution of this conflict in equality and harmony cannot be found in these chapters [of Genesis] but looks forward to a future redemption."[9]

There is no suggestion of a desirable hierarchy in Genesis 1–3. The focus is on equality in the image of God, and on co-stewardship, intimacy, unity, and love. That's the *true* "order of creation" we see in this passage, and it's *not* in any way hierarchical! To make these passages about women being in submission to men as part of "a created order" is to engage in *eisegesis*: to impose one's own convictions or theology on the Bible, instead of allowing the original meaning to be understood and to speak for itself.

Complementarians like to say that Genesis 1–3 supports their position that women were subordinate to men before the fall. But this is never stated in Genesis 1–3, and one can only arrive at that conclusion by superimposing their theology and worldview on these passages. These are complementarian *inferences* are usually made by Reformed theologians who are

---

9. Pierce et al., *Discovering Biblical Equality*, 94–95.

seeking to prop up their interpretation of a few Pauline texts. Genesis 1–3 never makes any claims about females being subordinate to males.

Paul draws on the creation account occasionally when making a theological point, but there should be no assumption that Paul is proposing a universal norm for behavior or interpretation, instead of a particular interpretation used to deal with a specific, time-bound problem. "Paul interprets Genesis, and Genesis in turn interprets Paul."[10] We come to Paul's discussion of "headship" later in this book. And I will make the case that Paul's words do not support a reading of Genesis 1–3 focused on hierarchy and subordination. Instead, Paul can be read in a way that aligns more closely with the words of Genesis 1–3 themselves. God made women and men for mutuality, equality, co-stewardship, intimacy, and to love and glorify God together, as full, and fully dignified and equal, partners.

The fact is that almost all modern Old Testament scholars (except for those committed to complementarianism) agree that Genesis 1–3 proposes the full dignity and equality of women and men—a beautiful, equal partnership, characterized by unity, difference, love, co-stewardship, and intimacy with God and each other. Pay careful attention! All the best modern, Christian, evangelical scholarship agrees on this point. Only complementarians disagree, and that's because their interpretation of Pauline passages becomes very weak once they concede this point.

Kevin Giles says that a rule does emerge from Genesis 1–3 and it is this:

> *All texts that imply or speak of the substantial and essential equality of the two sexes reflect the creation-given ideal; all texts that imply or speak of the subordination of women reflect the fall. They are not the God-given ideal. They either mirror the culture of the time or give practical time-bound advice to women living in a world where their subordination is assumed, or address an exceptional situation where the behavior of some women is causing offence.* All evangelicals who want to uphold the theological unity of Scripture should be pleased to embrace this rule.[11]

---

10. Westfall, *Paul and Gender*, 62.

11. Giles, *What the Bible Actually Teaches on Women*, 67.

SURVEYING THE BACKGROUND TO PAUL'S TEACHING ON WOMEN AND MEN

The writings of Paul the apostle—and especially a very few verses—are often cited as a prohibition on women teaching and leading in the church. But does that reading do justice to what Paul was saying?

Any competent reading and interpretation of the Bible always considers at least four contexts.

1. *Biblical*—What issues are being addressed by the author of this book of the Bible? What did the author mean to communicate to the recipients of the letter or book? What answers does the author give to specific problems addressed in the pages of that book? How do these verses fit into the overall argument and themes of this book? What is going on in the verses immediately preceding and following the verses we are looking at? Remember, "A text without a context is just a pretext for what we want it to mean."[12]

2. *Literary*—What kind of genre is this book, and how should we interpret this specific type of literature? There are sixty-six books in the Bible. They were written in a wide range of literary genres. These include narratives, law, poetry, wisdom sayings, prophecy, gospels, parables, epistles, and apocalyptic. The types of literature we have in front of us in a particular book of the Bible makes a big difference to how we read and apply it.

3. *Historical-cultural*—What do we know about the historical and cultural issues the original audience faced? This may include false teaching. But it also includes cultural norms, family structures, household codes, gender roles, surrounding cults and myths, tensions between Jewish and gentile believers, and much more. How is the author of this book seeking to address the historical-cultural problems and opportunities facing the original audience? Remember, reading a letter of Paul is like listening to one side of a phone conversation. We need to work very hard to understand the theological, historical, and cultural issues he was responding to, and which the original ancient audience were asking him for help with. We can often understand what a Bible passage is saying by simply reading it at face value. But that's not always the case. The words come to us from a culture that existed

12. Witherington, *Indelible Image*, 41.

thousands of years ago. Many of the words, ideas, customs, and so on are completely foreign to us. There are many instances where we only understand a passage by diving into the historical and cultural background. Learning about the ancient culture can help us better understand what is being said in this ancient text.

4.   *Contemporary*—How do we apply the insights and instructions of this ancient book or letter in our contemporary culture? What factors in our culture influence how we read this book, and what we see and don't see in its pages? What do we fail to see and understand in these pages that believers from another culture or time would clearly see? How does our culture and denominational or theological tradition influence us (both in positive and negative ways) as we read and apply this text? How do these words lead us toward love for Jesus, faithfulness to the gospel, and accurate biblical interpretation? What does it mean to apply these words in a courageous way that glorifies God?

These principles are important as we seek to understand the meaning and background to Paul's teaching on women and men.

Let's look at four key things that sit in the background of Paul's teachings on this topic.

The first is *Hellenistic culture* and Paul's own background.

The second is *household codes* and Christian witness.

The third is *heresies* and false teaching.

The fourth is the crucial and background *biblical issues* that inform our understanding of Paul's words.

1. Hellenistic Culture and Paul's Own Background

Paul had a Hellenistic and Jewish cultural and religious background. He was also heavily influenced by his teacher, Gamaliel. While some wealthier women forged good lives in first-century Hellenistic culture, it was still a culture with a strong misogynist streak. Men were considered superior to women, whose primary role was providing sexual gratification for men, bearing children, and looking after the home. Women were treated as the property of their husbands. Women lacked formal education, and were often excluded from learning and from the intellectual discourse and jargon of politics, society, and religion.

Philip Payne notes how new movements promoting equality for women were emerging in Paul's day. First-century Roman law was also beginning to change in order to give women many more rights. But pagan cults encouraged not only women's rights but also sexual freedoms and immorality. "This left Paul with a thorny problem: How could women demonstrate Christian liberty and equality in Christ without bringing offense to the gospel? He does this by honoring women as fully human even though this clashed with cultural conventions, and he affirms prophecy by women if done with modest deportment (1 Cor. 11:4–5)."[13]

Paul was taught by the famous Rabban Gamaliel I (the Elder). Gamaliel had a favorable view of women "in sharp contrast to the rabbinic tradition as a whole."[14] The sayings that survive from Gamaliel explicitly treat women and men equally. "None are derogatory toward women," and Gamaliel explicitly rejects the misogyny and mistreatment of women in his day. "Gamaliel's affirmations of women and his unusually free spirit, combined with the affinities of Paul to his great teacher, should caution against assuming that Paul shared the lowly view of women that characterized much of Pharisaic Judaism."[15]

Hellenistic culture, Greco-Roman society, and Pharisaic Judaism all treated women as inferior. The broad picture is that women were seen as sexual objects, useful for sexual gratification, childbearing, and raising children, and possessed an untrustworthy, weak, irrational nature. Paul's great teacher Gamaliel rejected these views. Paul's Lord and Savior Jesus Christ rejected these views. Paul himself rejected these views as well.

2. Household Codes and Christian Witness

The Pauline passages on women and men are closely associated with household codes, and with the broader witness of the Christian church in its society.

Cynthia Long Westfall points out that we need to understand a few key things about the Greco-Roman culture Paul is writing within. First, this is *an honor and shame culture*. Honor for men comes through their status in society (birth, wealth, class, privilege, etc.), their role in society (profession, influence, etc.), and their consequential sense of status and identity. Honor for women comes through their virtue and embodiment of female qualities

13. Payne, *Man and Woman, One in Christ*, 34–35.
14. Payne, *Man and Woman, One in Christ*, 36.
15. Payne, *Man and Woman, One in Christ*, 37.

(virginity, modesty, chastity, deferential behavior, loyalty, and mother-hood). Paul understands that the Christian witness is very much linked to these dynamics of honor and shame within this ancient culture.[16]

Second, this is a *patron-client culture.* Patronage is about the mutual exchange of goods and services for the common good (and often for social standing and advancement). Husbands and wives are usually unequal in this arrangement—the husband is the patron-benefactor and the wife is the inferior party. A woman's behavior and virtue are her responsibility in this arrangement, and the patron-benefactor (the husband) has most of the power, wealth, status, and control. As a "recipient of his care," the wife's responsibility is to return to him "respect, public praise, and loyal service, honoring him particularly through her obedience and chastity."[17]

Third, Paul is acutely aware that the way in which Christian women and men navigate these cultural expectations *will affect the public witness of the church* in Greco-Roman culture. This is where things like head coverings (1 Cor 11:3–16) and household codes come in. Take head coverings, for example. There was some confusion in the Corinthian church about whether women should wear head coverings while prophesying and praying, especially since they were often meeting in private homes. Paul instructs them to continue wearing head coverings, as a signal of their virtue, modesty, and domesticity. Corinth was a location known for sexual immorality, and the Christians must avoid the appearance of immorality at all costs. "In summary for that culture, a woman's hair represents her feminine beauty, and the way she dressed her hair represents her honor. Beauty and honor both reflect the range of meaning of δόξα ("glory") and allow for Paul's extensive wordplay in the passage. Covering hair in public represented modesty, honor, status, and protection for a woman, and an uncovered head in public disgraced a woman and put her sexually at risk."[18]

Paul's focus in 1 Cor 11:3–16 is not the relative status of women and men. His focus is on the glory of God, and his overall concern is the public reputation and witness of the church in Corinth. The women may, in fact, have been resisting taking off their head coverings, even though some church leaders were encouraging them to do so. Paul's "focus and concern are not reinforcing or increasing the authority or control of husbands over their wives, but rather ensuring that God is glorified, that the women are

16. Westfall, *Paul and Gender*, 18–19.

17. Westfall, *Paul and Gender*, 21–22.

18. Westfall, *Paul and Gender*, 30–31.

not personally disgraced or shamed while they pray and prophesy, and that they not send out an inappropriate message through their dress by displaying their hair while they minister and worship. If women were resisting taking off their head coverings, Paul was supporting them, their judgment, and their honor within the house church and within the community, possibly even against the church leadership."[19] The focus is on God's glory and on credible Christian witness.

Some of the New Testament household codes were borrowed from Greco-Roman culture. The household codes prescribe the order of relations between various members of households: husbands, wives, masters, slaves, and children (see Col 3:18—4:1; Eph 5:22—6:9; 1 Tim 2:9–15; Titus 2:2–10; 1 Pet 2:13—3:7). These biblical household codes seem to appropriate Greco-Roman and first-century Jewish cultures, yet liberalize them in striking ways, while paying attention to Christian morality, public witness, and the example and words of Jesus. These codes were far from ideal, but they helped in a setting where the church was under threat and meeting secretly behind closed doors. The Christians wanted to ensure that they were seen to be commendable and upright in conduct, virtue, and honor. The challenge for the modern reader is what to do with these ancient household codes? How do we apply ancient Greco-Roman household codes to modern families?

I want to avoid the impression that I think the Christian household codes are merely some kind of accommodation to Greco-Roman culture, or some kind of survival strategy in the face of real threats to their survival. David Starling warns against this, and says we should not miss that the rationales given for these relationships and behaviors are distinctly Christian. Paul appeals to "the intentions of the creator, interpreted in the light of Old Testament Scripture and its fulfilment in the gospel of Christ."[20]

Starling says we should reject the view that these household codes are "timeless ethical templates" (the words about slaves and masters should make us realize that this can't be the case, for instance). Starling says we should also reject the view that these codes are mere cultural accommodations and not really what Paul believed (the fact that Paul offers no accommodationist rationale, and offers, instead, deeply theological rationales, should make us realize that this can't be the full story).

---

19. Westfall, *Paul and Gender*, 42.

20. Murphy and Starling, *Gender Conversation*, 74.

The challenge, then, is to wrestle with the cultural contingencies of the household codes (slaves and masters is just one example), while perceiving and honoring the theological and ethical themes that undergird them. What are these themes (present in the code and in the texts that surround them)? Glorify God. Preserve the gospel. Act ethically. Be unified and mature. Love God and his church and your neighbors. Follow the example of Christ. Enjoy freedom expressed through Christian virtue and discipleship. Be self-disciplined and maintain order. Love one another, and practice mutual submission out of reverence for Christ. Be reconciled through Christ. Cultivate spiritual gifts. Be godly and holy. Worship and praise God for your living hope. The list goes on!

So, here's my modest proposal for how we interpret and apply the household codes today, in our cultural context:

1.   Understand that they were shaped within a particular culture, to meet the demands and expectations of that culture. We can't escape the extent of their cultural contingencies.

2.   Don't dismiss their relevance today, though, on that basis. Paul gives good theological reasons for many of these household codes.

3.   Seek the major theological and ethical themes that inform and undergird these household codes.

4.   Ask which of these household codes can be lived out today while doing the following:

    a.   Honoring these foundational ethical themes;

    b.   Supporting the broader canonical witness, including the words and example of Jesus Christ himself;

    c.   Preserving Christian witness in our cultural context;

    d.   Maintaining the godliness, orderliness, and holiness of the Christian community.

5.   Always keep three things in mind as we seek to interpret and apply the household codes today: First, how are we glorifying God in this? Second, how are we preserving the truth of the gospel? Third, how are we advancing the witness and holiness of the church?

3. Heresies and False Teaching

Heresies and false teaching in the first-century churches (and their surrounding cultures) is the third thing we must consider as we survey the background to Paul's teaching on women and men.

The heresy in the Ephesian church is just one example. Paul was writing to Timothy for a number of reasons, and one was to deal with this Ephesian heresy (1 Tim 1:3–4a). Many scholars propose that the Ephesian cult of Artemis had infiltrated the Ephesian church. In a helpful blog post titled, "1 Timothy 2:12 in Context: The Heresy in the Ephesian Church," Margaret Mowczko outlines some of the heresies threatening the Ephesian church.[21] These included the syncretizing of Christian with pagan religions (the cult of Artemis, for example) and the influence of Christian Gnosticism. These false teachings encouraged strange myths, endless genealogies, abstinence from certain foods, weird theologies about Jesus and the resurrection, bizarre interpretations of the Genesis creation accounts, and refraining from marriage.

Philip Payne offers a brilliant exegetical study of "the many close parallels between Paul's description of the false teachers and of women in the Ephesian church."[22] Payne explains how this shows that the women in the Ephesian church had been strongly influenced by heretical beliefs. Ephesian Christian women had been deceived by false teachers. Even three strong advocates for complementarianism acknowledge this: Moo, Mounce, and Schreiner. Philip Payne concludes,

> First Timothy's many statements regarding problems caused by women depict a situation where women had become central to the false teaching that was dividing the church. The evidence for this is so strong that it has led three of the most prominent advocates that 1 Tim 2.12 forever prohibits women from teaching or having authority over men to acknowledge, respectively: "The false teachers had persuaded many women to follow them in their doctrines (1 Tim 5.15; 2 Tim 3.6–7)"; the text "explicitly pictures only women as being influenced by the heresy"; and "it is likely that the prohibition [1 Tim 2.12] is given because some women were teaching men." The occasion that elicited the particular statements in 1 Tim 2:11–15 is important for understanding both what Paul was prohibiting and the reasoning he gives for it.[23]

21. See Mowczko, "1 Timothy 2:12 In Context: The Heresy in the Ephesian Church."

22. Payne, *Man and Woman, One in Christ*, 300.

23. Payne, *Man and Woman, One in Christ*, 304.

4. Biblical Issues that Inform Our Understanding of Paul's Words

Finally, we must also look at the background *biblical issues* that inform our understanding of Paul's words. These inform our interpretation of Paul, and include:

1. The words and life of Jesus and the example he set for Paul and the church

2. A theology of Genesis and the created order

3. Paul's practice of honoring and releasing female leaders in the churches

4. The many examples of women in leadership in the Old and New Testaments

Since we've already looked at numbers one and two on that list, let's turn now to biblical issues three and four.

OUTLINING PAUL'S PRACTICE OF HONORING AND RELEASING WOMEN TO TEACH AND LEAD

Paul had a service-focused and charismatic view of leadership and ministry. For Paul, all ministry is an act of service in the imitation of our servant Lord. And all ministry flows from God's empowering presence, as he distributes his gifts to whomever he chooses. 1 Cor 12–14; Rom 12:3–8; and Eph 4:11–12 give us a wonderful insight into Paul's theology of leadership.

"Now to each one the manifestation of the Spirit is given for the common good" (1 Cor 12:7). The Spirit is God's empowering presence. The spirit of Jesus Christ pours out God's gifts on the whole church, on every believer, so that the whole church might be built up in Christ, and released into ministry and mission. All this is for the glory of God, and so that all people might believe in Jesus Christ and be saved. We will come back to the theme of God's empowering Spirit later in this book. But I am concerned that scholars do not make enough mention of Paul's charismatic understanding of ministry when they discuss the theme of women in ministry. For me, Paul's theology of the Spirit and of charismatic, service-shaped ministry are central to the discussion on who is qualified to lead and minister in Christ's church. More on that topic soon.

One of the many reasons I believe that Paul's words do *not* prohibit women from public teaching and Christian leadership is because Paul himself released women to serve and lead. This is one of the reasons why I believe that 1 Tim 2:8–15 is dealing with a specific problem at Ephesus, and *not* making a universal prohibition on women teaching and leading. *Many* other passages lead us to believe that women can serve and lead on the same basis as men. And Paul encouraged women to lead, serve, and teach in the churches. So there *must* be something special about the situation in Ephesus that led Paul to say this.

Kevin Giles puts it this way,

> Paul's *practice* of ministry reflects closely his *theology* of ministry. The number of women in leadership in the early Pauline churches, given the cultural context, is breathtaking. Nowhere is this more obvious than in the sixteenth chapter of his epistle to the Romans. In this final chapter, he mentions ten women; he names eight of them, and commends the ministry and leadership of seven. Most of them were almost certainly women of some social standing. If we consider all the early Paulines more than one-quarter of the leaders Paul mentions by name are women, twelve in number.[24]

Let's list out the women Paul honors and names in ministry and leadership. It's clear that Paul made a practice of honoring and releasing women to serve, teach, evangelize, and lead.

In his epistles [Paul] speaks explicitly and positively of—

- Women prophets (1 Cor. 11:5, c.f. Acts 2:17, 21:9). And for him the prophet is "second" in the church, the teacher "third" (1 Cor. 12:22) and he says prophecy is a ministry of first importance because it builds up the church (1 Cor. 14:1–13).

- A woman apostle (Rom 16:7), "first in the church" (1 Cor. 12:28).

- Women church workers and evangelists (Rom. 16:6, 12, Phil. 4:3).

- Women as "fellow workers" in the Gospel (Rom. 16:3, Phil. 4:2–3).

- Women as leaders of house churches (Col. 4:15, 1 Cor. 1:11, c.f. Acts 12:12, 16:14–15, 40 etc.).

- Women deacons (Rom. 16:1, 1 Tim. 2:9).

- Husband and wife ministry teams (Acts 18:24–28, Rom. 16:7).

Given the patriarchal cultural setting, the number of women involved in Christian le\adership in the first-century church is quite

---

24. Giles, *What the Bible Actually Teaches on Women*, 98.

amazing. What this evidence means is that *the apostolic practice of ministry* wherever possible *matched the apostolic theology of ministry.* These examples show that Paul valued women in a way none but his Lord and master had done.[25]

Kevin Giles offers a useful summary of the women Paul mentions in leadership and ministry. Here's a summary.

Phoebe—Romans 16:1–2

Paul commends Phoebe in Rom 16:1–2. He calls her a *diakonis* and a *prostatis. Diakonis* is the feminine form of *diakonoi* (deacon) and its equivalent. Who else does Paul call *diakonoi?* None other than himself, Apollos, Tychicus, Epaphras, and Timothy. She was clearly a highly regarded church leader. She is also a *prostatis*, which is the only time this word is used in the New Testament. It means "to stand before." The word was used at the time of prominent leaders, presidents of associations, and patrons of high social standing. Shortly before Paul uses this word, he speaks of "those in leadership" and uses a version of this word to do so (*ho proistamenous*). Phoebe was a deacon, with high social standing in the churches, and exercising senior leadership. We also know that deacons were expected to teach the gospel and the Scriptures publicly.

Priscilla—Romans 16:3–5

Priscilla and Aquila worked together for the expansion of first-century Christianity. Paul speaks of them in Rom 16:3–5. They were a missionary marriage of great note! Priscilla even instructed the great Christian teacher Apollos. Some try to discount this by suggesting that Priscilla instructed Apollos privately—but Paul does not say this. Paul says that Priscilla and Aquila instructed Apollos, and there's no reason to believe this wasn't in a public setting, especially given Priscilla and Aquila had prominent leadership in the churches. Paul calls both Priscilla and Aquila *sunergoi* (fellow workers or coworkers). Paul didn't just have men in "the Pauline circle" of leaders—Priscilla was among them.

25. Giles, "Paul and Women."

Junia—Romans 16:7

Junia was almost certainly a woman apostle (Rom 16:7). She was a second-generation apostle, if you will, along with Barnabas, Apollos, James, and Timothy. Some try to argue that it's better to call her a missionary or a church planter. But whatever title you use (and I think Paul prefers *apostle* in this passage!) she was clearly teaching, preaching, and leading God's people in a very public way. She was "a sent one" like the other apostles. Some try to argue that you can translate this verse as Junia being esteemed *by* the apostles (instead of serving *as* one of the apostles). But virtually all modern scholars agree that "in this context the Greek most naturally means that Junia and Andronicus are commended by Paul as esteemed apostles."[26]

Eldon Epp concludes: "It remains a fact that there was a woman apostle, explicitly so named, in the earliest generation of Christianity, and contemporary Christians—laypeople and clergy—must (and eventually will) face up to it."[27]

Other Women Co-Laborers

When honoring women in ministry, Paul doesn't stop there!

He speaks of other women as co-laborers in the gospel. Mary, Tryphaena, Tryphosa, and Persis labor in the gospel (Rom 16:6, 12). By the way, the Greek term Paul uses (*kopiao*) is the one he uses consistently of his own labor of preaching and teaching. He uses this word consistently in that way; such that it is almost certain that these women labored (*kopiao*) in preaching and teaching just as he did.

In Phil 4:3, Paul speaks of Euodia and Syntyche as *sunergoi*—fellow workers or coworkers. Paul only calls a few of his most trusted friends and fellow leaders *sunergoi*—Clement, Epaphroditus, Timothy, and Titus. Paul puts these two women (Euodia and Syntyche) right up there with these men.

Paul keeps going! He speaks positively about both women and men prophesying in the churches, a role that was just as public and important as teaching (1 Cor 11:4–5). Prophets had a very senior and public role in the churches, and one can only get around the fact that women exercised

---

26. Giles, *What the Bible Actually Teaches on Women*, 102.

27. Epp, *Junia*, 81.

this role by somehow trying to downplay the importance of the role itself—which Paul never does!

Paul also mentions women who were house church leaders, a pastoral and teaching role that was primary in the first-century church—Lydia (Acts 17:11–15), Nympha (Col 4:15), and very likely Chloe (1 Cor 1:11). Priscilla and Aquila led a house church together (Rom 16:5; 1 Cor 16:19). Acts also mentions the women who are mentioned as the founding pillars of the churches of Thessalonica and Berea (Acts 17:4, 12).

Going through the long list of women in ministry whom Paul mentions and honors, Philip Payne, Kevin Giles, Michael Bird, N. T. Wright, Gordon Fee, Scot McKnight, Klyne Snodgrass, Margaret Mowczko, yours truly, and many others conclude that Paul's affirmation for women in ministry is undeniable.

This affirmation of women teaching and leading fits with the guiding influences on his life: "the Holy Scriptures, Gamaliel, Jesus, and the Holy Spirit."[28] Payne goes on to show how Paul's theological convictions "provide the framework for understanding his teachings about man and woman . . . [These] firmly imply the equal standing of men and women."[29]

According to Philip Payne (and I believe he is right!), here are the "theological axioms" that Paul holds. Each is offered here in Payne's own words. Each of the twelve imply the equality of women and men in Christ:

1. Male and female are equally created in God's image (Col 3:10; 2 Cor 3:18)

2. Male and female equally received the creation mandate and blessing (Gen 1:26–30; 1 Tim 6:17; 1 Cor 10:23–30)

3. The redeemed—male and female—are equally "in Christ" (Rom 10:12–13; Gal 3:28; 1 Cor 11:11)

4. The nature of church leadership as service applies equally to male and female (1 Cor 1–2; Rom 1:1; 1 Cor 9:19; Gal 1:10; 1 Cor 16:16; Matt 20:25–28; Luke 22:25–27)

5. Mutual submission in the church presupposes the equal standing of women and men (Eph 5:18–21; 1 John 4:13; Gal 5:13; Rom 12:10; Eph 4:2)

28. Payne, *Man and Woman, One in Christ*, 68.

29. Payne, *Man and Woman, One in Christ*, 69.

6. Mutual submission in marriage presupposes the equality of men and women (Eph 5:21–22; Col 3:18–19; Titus 2:4)

7. The oneness of the body of Christ presupposes the equality of men and women (1 Cor 12:25)

8. The priesthood of all believers presupposes the equality of men and women (2 Cor 3:12–18; Col 3:16; 1 Cor 14:26)

9. The gifts of the Spirit manifest the equality of men and women (1 Cor 12:7; Rom 12:6–8; 1 Cor 12:11, 31; 14:1)

10. Liberty in Christ presupposes the equality of men and women (Gal 3:28; 5:1; 1 Thess 2:7)

11. Inaugurated eschatology requires the equality of men and women while affirming that the sexes complement each other (1 Cor 7; 1 Tim 4:3; Eph 2:11–22, etc.)

12. In Christ, male and female are equal (Gal 3:28; Jas 2:1–13).[30]

Unsurprisingly, Paul's practice of honoring and releasing women to serve and lead is matched by his theology.

CELEBRATING THE EXAMPLES OF WOMEN IN LEADERSHIP IN THE OLD AND NEW TESTAMENTS

The stories of Phoebe, Priscilla, and Junia are remarkable. As we've seen, Paul mentions many other women leaders in the church. This affirmation of women as leaders accords with his theological convictions and ministry practices. The Gospels make much of women in service to our Lord too. Mary of Bethany was a disciple who "sat at Jesus's feet" in the tradition of all those who sat at the teacher's feet in order to become teachers themselves (Luke 10:38–42). We see stories of other female disciples, such as Joanna (the manager of Herod's household), Mary Magdalene, Susanna, and more.

A guiding principle for understanding a Bible text is that the conclusions which we draw from one text must correlate and agree with the rest of Scripture. A complementarian understanding of 1 Tim 2:11–15 makes synthesis impossible.

---

30. Payne, *Man and Woman, One in Christ*, ch. 3.

The Scriptures illustrate that ministry flows from quality of character and the gifts given, not from gender. To each a ministry is given (Acts 2:17–18; Rom 12:3–8; 1 Cor 12:7–11; Eph 4:7; 1 Pet 4:10–11).

The stories of Phoebe, Priscilla, and Junia aren't the only accounts we should recognize and commend. As the "Spirit is poured out on all flesh, and your sons and your daughters prophesy" (Acts 2:17–18) we see many examples of the Spirit emboldening and propelling women into public leadership, teaching, and ministry. We see this throughout the Old and New Testaments. We should celebrate these stories!

The Old Testament contains many women who functioned in positions of leadership and responsibility. Miriam was recognized as a leader alongside Moses; a spiritual leader and a prophet (Mic 6:4; Exod 15:20–21). Deborah was one of Israel's judges, and, as Scot McKnight points out, clearly a presidential leader (Judg 4:4–6).[31] Noadiah was a prophet (Neh 6:14). Huldah was a prophet. In fact, she was a "prophet above the prophets." King Josiah chooses to seek guidance that will lead the nation to repentance and a fresh commitment to God's covenant. Who does he consult? He could have called on Jeremiah, Zephaniah, Nahum, Habakkuk, or Huldah. He chooses the female prophet, Huldah, to help lead the nation back to Yahweh (2 Kgs 22:8–20; 2 Chron 34:19–28). Scot McKnight says, "Huldah was not chosen because no men were available; she is chosen because she is truly exceptional among the prophets."[32] Anna, in the Gospel of Luke, was also a prophet (Luke 2:36–38). Other prominent Old Testament women included Ruth, Esther, Sarah, Rebekah, and Rahab.

In the New Testament we see examples of women in various leadership roles. Junia was almost certainly a female apostle—most Protestant New Testament scholars today agree on this point (Rom 16:7). There were women prophets (Luke 2:36; Acts 2:17; 21:9; 1 Cor 11:5), women deacons (Rom 16:1), women house church leaders (Col 4:15), and husband and wife leadership teams (Acts 18:24–28; Rom 16:7). Jesus himself displayed equality of consideration and honor for women and men (Mark 12:40; Luke 8:2; 10:39; 13:10–16; 23:27; John 4:27). For a great summary of New Testament women church leaders, see Margaret Mowczko's blog post "Women Church Leaders in the New Testament."[33]

---

31. McKnight, *Blue Parakeet*, 168–74.

32. McKnight, *Blue Parakeet*, 174.

33. Mowczko, "Women Church Leaders in the New Testament."

Stanley Grenz notes that the gospel "radically altered the position of women, elevating them to a partnership with men unparalleled in first-century society."[34]

The entire Scriptures show that God takes delight in seeing women function in ministry to his people. From the examples above it is obvious that there were many women teachers and leaders. (The role of male and female prophets, for instance, was a senior role in the church. It's hard to argue that prophecy is any less important than teaching—some Pauline texts indicate that it is at least as important. And the house church leader is very similar to that of a pastor-teacher in many respects, with house church leaders being the ancient equivalent of today's pastor-teachers.)

Women exercised leadership and ministry gifts throughout the Old and New Testaments. I see no advantage at all in trying to explain these examples away. On the contrary, we should be celebrating and honoring these women and their service to God and his people!

WRESTLING WITH THE KEY PAULINE AND OTHER PASSAGES

A small group of Pauline passages are usually consulted in the discussion about what the Bible teaches on men and women, and what roles women can perform in the church. I turn to these passages now, asking two questions. What do they actually teach on women and men? How should we then apply their insights and instructions today?

Galatians 3:28

There is neither Jew nor Gentile, neither slave nor free, nor is there male and female, for you are all one in Jesus Christ. (Gal 3:28)

This important verse has become something of the evangelical egalitarian manifesto. But we need to be careful to interpret and apply it accurately. Paul isn't talking about ministry in this verse. He's talking about being one in Christ. He's focusing on equality in salvation and among the family of God. Jesus Christ has made one family out of the two. All who believe in Christ are now part of this one family: men, women, slaves, free, Jews, and

---

34. Grenz and Kjesbo, *Women in the Church*, 78.

gentiles. Our belief in Jesus Christ makes us one, unified, countercultural, redeemed family. "So in Christ Jesus you are all children of God through faith, for all of you who were baptized into Christ have clothed yourselves with Christ" (Gal 3:26–27). This is the family God promised to Abraham. This one new family is now revealed—by the power of the Spirit and to the glory of God—in Jesus Christ.

Paul isn't arguing for the abolishment of the created order. He isn't arguing for a genderless church where women and men are undifferentiated. (He also never argues for the obliteration of cultural and ethnic differences between Jews and gentiles.) The new creation in Jesus Christ does not abolish the old creation, including God's creation of male and female in Genesis 1–3. Paul never discounts the differences between the sexes and the unique contributions that each make. In contrast to the gnostics, Paul elevates the body and honors the genders and their differences. Instead, what Paul is doing here is countering the Judaizing influences on the Galatian church that sought to privilege Jews and males. The Judaizers were trying to establish the ceremonial customs of the Jewish law, including circumcision, which would have effectively excluded women, gentiles, and slaves from full participation in worship and other aspects of the life of the church. They especially emphasized the importance of circumcision. Paul says, no, you are now one in Christ, and women and men are brought together as equally and completely as Jews and gentiles. All are equally honored in the family of Jesus Christ. All the barriers separating you and keeping you from being one body in love and worship are now done away with in Christ. You are freed from the bondage of the law.

Scot McKnight writes,

> Many things can be said, have been said, and will be said about this verse. It both carries far too much weight for some and scares the traditions of others. I offer only a few observations:
>
> 1. To distinguish between soteriology (access to God) and ecclesiology (what one can do in church) cannot be sustained by this verse. For Paul, ethnic, socio-economic (class), and gender divisions are broken down because what Paul is claiming here fulfills OT expectations.
>
> 2. The theme of the immediate verses is not about soteriology but about *unity*—that each of these groups is brought into a new family—hence, the fundamental orientation is about *ecclesiology* and not simply soteriology.

3. Identity changes in Christ: one's identity is no longer simply ethnic, socio-economic or gender but what one is in the new family in Christ. This does not obliterate any of these realities—Paul sustains ethnic difference in 1 Cor 7 etc. It eliminates these realities as boundaries between people and with God.

4. The most significant OT background to this text is not Genesis 1:27 (male and female) but New Creation themes found in Isa 2:1–5; 25:6–8; 51:4; 66:19–21; Mic 4:2–5; Zech 14:16; and Joel 2:28–32; 3:1–5. These themes are developed by Paul in 2 Cor 5:14–17 and also at Gal 6:15. I suggest the following ideas feed into Gal 3:28:

   a. The eschatological gathering of all to *worship* the one true God together.

   b. *God will gift all people*—ethnic, socio-economic, and gender—with God's Spirit so that all will be gifted to ministry. Notice Joel 2:28–29 as background to Gal 3:28: "And afterward, I will pour out my Spirit on all people. Your sons and daughters will prophesy, your old men will dream dreams, your young men will see visions. Even on my servants, both men and women, I will pour out my Spirit in those days."[35]

This passage has social implications for slaves and free persons. It has social implications for Jews and gentiles. Why would we not think that it has social implications for women and men? It must. Those who seek to restrict the meaning of Gal 3:28 to a "spiritual standing and unity" deny the power of this passage, and the way in which these Pauline convictions actually shaped the early churches. Moreover, everyone in the ancient world knew that religious and gender distinctions have social implications. Paul says that the old (and anti-gospel) divisions and hierarchies, the destructive power plays and superiorities, and the toxic prejudices and fears, are now to be put away! Get rid of them! You are now all one in Jesus Christ. You are all equally valued, equally loved, equally honored, and equally a part of his family.

So, how did Paul practice the social implications of his theological convictions expressed in Gal 3:28? He fought for the right of gentiles to enjoy full participation and ministry in the life of the church (Gal 2:11–14). He invited women to become honored coworkers, and, as we have seen, welcomed them into senior leadership roles in the churches (Rom 16:1–16).

---

35. McKnight, "Women in Ministry: Galatians 3:28."

Paul isn't content to give lip service to equality and unity. His practices of honoring and promoting women align with his theology.

Ronald W. Pierce asks some important questions: "Can we acknowledge that Paul in his letter to the Galatians does not qualify his inclusion of women as fully functioning members of the New Covenant community? Gentiles and slaves are welcomed in today's churches at all levels of participation without restriction—why not women?"[36]

The only reason why we would exclude women from full participation in service and leadership is because of our interpretation of a few verses, which we will turn to soon. We will see that those verses do not have to be read the way complementarians read them. An alternative reading—one which honors Jesus's vision of biblical equality—is possible. The egalitarian reading that I propose is more in line with the radical biblical vision of one new people in Christ, articulated by Paul in Gal 3:28.

1 Corinthians 7

The husband does not have authority over his body, but his wife does. (1 Cor 7:4)

A husband must not leave his wife. (7:11)

The unbelieving husband has been sanctified through his wife. (7:14)

As I read through 1 Corinthians 7 again I am struck by what an astonishingly egalitarian and countercultural chapter this is. In contrast to the norms of the surrounding Greco-Roman culture, Paul says that women and men have equal rights in marriage. We sometimes miss how remarkable—no, astonishing!—these words would have seemed to first-century Greco-Roman ears.

In this chapter, Paul says that women and men have the same rights, obligations, conditions, expectations, and honor as each other, in at least thirteen distinct issues in marriage (verses 2–5, 10–16, 28, 32–34, 39). Those issues are:

Freedom for both women and men to have a believing spouse.

The importance for both women and men to honor fidelity in marriage.

Mutual honor in sexual relations.

36. Pierce, *Partners in Marriage and Ministry*, 43.

Shared marital duties and equal spousal rights.

Shared relinquishment of authority over one's own body.

Mutual sexual consent and mutual consent for abstinence.

A command to men and women not to separate, but to seek reconciliation.

Shared responsibilities regarding divorce and staying together.

Both women and men can sanctify an unbelieving spouse.

Freedom for both women and men to remarry if an unbelieving spouse leaves.

Freedom for both genders to marry or not to marry.

Freedom for both men and women to remarry if a spouse dies.

Both women and men can enjoy devotion to ministry.

In Greco-Roman culture, most women were treated as inferior, as sexual objects, and as the property of their husbands. They had little or no rights in their marriages. As I've said before, it is surprising that every woman in the first-century Roman Empire didn't convert to Christianity, when you look at the freedoms, dignity, equality, and honor that Christianity offered them. Paul says things in this passage that would have sounded shocking and revolutionary to ancient ears. "The husband does not have authority over his body, but his wife does" (7:4). "A husband must not leave his wife" (7:11). "The unbelieving husband has been sanctified through his wife" (7:14). These words are in stark contrast to the values and practices of Paul's age, and show how much he honored and elevated women.

The symmetry of Paul's expressions in this passage reinforce the theme of equality and mutuality. Men and women are addressed equally—as are their equal responsibilities and rights—through symmetrical words and phrases. Furthermore, Paul makes it clear that a woman's value isn't dependent on whether she marries or does not marry (7:34).

We modern readers can sometimes miss the power of a chapter like 1 Corinthians 7. In this chapter, Paul offers a vision of Christian marriage and gender relations marked by equality and mutuality in Christ.

1 Corinthians 11:2–16

But I want you to realize that the head of every man is Christ, and the head of the woman is man, and the head of Christ is God. Every man who prays or prophesies with his head covered dishonors his head. But every woman who prays or prophesies with her head uncovered dishonors her head—it is the same as having her head shaved. For if a woman does not cover her head, she might as well have her hair cut off; but if it is a disgrace for a woman to have her hair cut off or her head shaved, then she should cover her head.

A man ought not to cover his head, since he is the image and glory of God; but woman is the glory of man. For man did not come from woman, but woman from man; neither was man created for woman, but woman for man. It is for this reason that a woman ought to have authority over her own head, because of the angels. Nevertheless, in the Lord woman is not independent of man, nor is man independent of woman. For as woman came from man, so also man is born of woman. But everything comes from God.

This is a complex passage. It's no wonder that there are strong disagreements among scholars about what it means. So, we need to tread carefully, recognizing the difficulties of understanding this passage.

Before we get into what Paul says about "head" and "head coverings," we should note that Paul mentions women publicly prophesying and praying in the Corinthian church. Women were involved in public ministry in the church, and Paul affirms this by not indicating in any way that they should stop. Paul does not discourage women from ministering publicly, but, instead, gives instructions for how men and women should conduct themselves in the public assembly. It's also worth noting that Paul says these things after discussing "the believer's freedoms in Christ," and our shared responsibility to seek the good of many, so that they may be saved (1 Cor 10:23—11:1).

Some complementarians, like the Köstenbergers, read 1 Cor 11:2–16 and conclude, "First Corinthians 11:2–16 teaches that a woman may participate in praying and prophesying in church *under male spiritual leadership and authority.*"[37] But I challenge you to read the chapter *without* this assumption, and see if the chapter actually says that. I've read the chapter over and over again, trying to see where Paul actually says such a thing, and it's just not there. The only reason you'd read the chapter this way is if you came to it with a particular axe to grind or theological position to maintain. Paul does say some things about *kephalē* ("head") which are difficult to interpret, but he never makes the point the Köstenbergers make.

---

37. Köstenberger and Köstenberger, *God's Design for Man and Woman*, 176.

1. What Does Paul Mean By Kephalē ("Head")?

Paul says, "But I want you to realize that the head of every man is Christ, and the head of every woman is man, and the head of Christ is God" (1 Cor 11:3). The question is, what does Paul mean by *kephalē* ("head") in these verses?

1 Corinthians 11:3 has often been used to demonstrate men's leadership or rulership over women, and therefore that women functioning in pastoral or teaching offices is inappropriate. The word "head" as used in this verse is a metaphorical term which we have often understood as meaning sovereign or ruler over. Our understanding of the function of the central nervous system is relatively new, and ancient writers therefore did not view the brain or the "head" as the primary director of the affairs of the body. To them the center and sovereign of bodily function was the "heart" (see the psalmist references to the "heart"). Therefore, we must approach 1 Cor 11:3 with considerable care so as not to attach our preconceived concepts of what it means to be "head" to the author's actual meaning.

Yet, sometimes, the word used for "head" here does mean "sovereign" or "ruler over" or "one who has authority over." So, we can't dispose of the possibility that it means this in 1 Corinthians 11 so easily.

The Hebrew word for "head" (*rosh*) is translated in the Septuagint (LXX) by about thirty different equivalents. The Old Testament attributes a variety of meanings to *rosh*. A primary usage is of the sources of rivers (Gen 2:10), of the beginning of months (Exod 12:2), and of the beginning of a street (Ezra 16:25). Therefore "head" (*rosh*) in Hebrew writings, and in particular the Old Testament, may be associated with a wide variety of meanings which do not specifically relate to dominance or rulership over something or someone. The Hebrew *rosh* has connotations of "source" or "origin."

The Greek word for "head" (*kephalē*) also has a considerable range of meanings. In Greek literature *kephalē* may often mean "authority over," however it may also mean "source" or "origin." Markus Barth in his work *Ephesians* lists Orphic fragments, Plato, Cleanthes's hymn to Zeus and other Stoics, the magic papyri, the Naassene sermon, and other documents right up to early medieval Mandean documents as using *kephalē* with the meaning of "originator, power source, and life splendor."[38] Barth states that "Old Testament and rabbinical physiological and medical ideas stand nearer the views of Aristotle and the Stoics" (i.e. viewing the heart as primarily leading the body) "than to Plato and the Platonizing natural scientists" (i.e. who

---

38. Barth, *Ephesians*, 185.

gave the preeminence to the brain).[39] It is very likely therefore that Paul, being thoroughly acquainted with and taught in Old Testament and rabbinical physiological and medical ideas, was speaking of man as the origin of woman rather than the authority over woman. G. W. H. Lampe's *A Patristic Greek Lexicon* has twenty-two lines of citations in support of the concept that *kephalē* in 1 Cor 11:3 is equivalent to *arche* (*arche* in Greek means "source" or "beginning"). But we should take note that scholars such as Richard S. Cervin disagree that *kephalē* and *arche* are equivalents (we'll come back to Cervin's work in a moment).

With terms such as "head of state" we have come to associate "head" as meaning superior and including a directing or governing function. The word *kephalē* occurs seventy-five times in the New Testament, and is used in a great variety of ways. Examples of the variety of meanings follow. "Lift up your heads" (Luke 21:28). "Your blood be on your own head" (Acts 18:6). "Not a hair of your head will perish" (Acts 27:34). "Heaping coals of fire on your enemy's head" (Rom 12:20). And "The head of the corner" in building (Mark 12:10; 1 Pet 2:7). Therefore, we must use great caution not to predetermine the meaning of the word "head" in any individual passage.

Many scholars say that it's wrong to assume that *kephalē* means "having authority over someone." Instead, *kephalē* carries the sense of "source," as in the "head of a river." As we've noted, Paul uses *kephalē* in different places to mean different things. Sometimes he means it in the sense of "authority" and other times he means it in the sense of "source." So, does Paul use *kephalē* ("head") in 1 Corinthians 11 to mean that men have authority over women? Or does he mean that men are the "source" of women, as in the Genesis account (Gen 2:21–22)?

"I want you to know that Christ is the head of every man and the man is head of woman and God is head of Christ" (1 Cor 11:3). If we come to the resolute conclusion that Paul the apostle is using "head" in the sense of "leading or supreme person" we run into difficulty with this verse. God is not the head of Christ in the same sense that Christ is the head of man, and man is not the head of woman in the same sense as either. Our concept of the doctrine of the Trinity does not allow us to consider the Father's headship as one of superiority or rulership. Christ's headship over every man does involve an element of superiority or rulership.

When we consider the relationship of man to woman in this verse, we must keep in mind the fact that "head" could mean an element of superiority

39. Barth, *Ephesians*, 189.

(as in Christ to man) or it could mean equality of relationship (as in God to Christ). However, if we return to our concept of *kephalē* meaning "source" or "origin" this verse makes absolute sense. God is the "source" of Christ in that he was begotten in the virgin Mary. Christ is the "source" of man in that Christ was involved in creation. Man is the "source" of woman in that Genesis tells us that Eve was called "woman, because she was taken out of man" (Gen 2:23). If we consider *kephalē* as possibly meaning "source" or "origin" then there is nothing in this text which hinders women from ministering in pastoral or teaching or prophetic roles (after all, Paul mentions women prophesying).

> It may be that, in applying the analogy of headship, the concept of subordination has wrongly been imported. "Head" here may rather have the sense of origin or fount of being. Indeed, Paul does not say that man is the lord (*kyrios*) of woman, he says that he is the origin of her being. Such an interpretation would also preserve us here from a false "subordinationism" whether between Father and Son, as running contrary to the orthodox doctrine of the Trinity, or between man and woman, as inappropriate since both are made in the divine image.[40]

2. Paul Explains the Meaning of Kephalē in Terms that Indicate "Source" or "Origin"

When Paul explains what he is saying (verses 8, 9, and 12a) he refers explicitly to the creation story in Genesis 2, where a woman is formed from the side of a man, who is, obviously, her "source." These references to Genesis give weight to an understanding of *kephalē* ("head") as meaning "source and origin."

Examining the ancient literature (biblical and other), Philip Payne offers fifteen compelling reasons why *kephalē* is best understood as "source" rather than "authority" in this passage. I won't list them all here, but it's a comprehensive, masterful, and convincing analysis. Payne goes into some depth into the ancient sources and Paul's writings. I encourage you to read his examination in these texts, and his arguments for viewing *kephalē* as "source."[41]

---

40. Anglican Advisory Council, *Ordination of Women to the Priesthood*, 26.

41. Payne, *Man and Woman, One in Christ*, 117–39.

3. Paul's Words Do Not Indicate Hierarchy or "Chain of Command"

Michael Bird also observes: "Importantly, Paul is not arguing here for a chain of command along the lines of God > Christ > Man > Woman. Note the order of the couplets as they appear: Christ/Man, then Husband/Wife, and finally God/Christ, which does not lend itself to a hierarchy from the Father at the top with women at the bottom."[42] Since Paul isn't describing a chain of command, it's again likely that he has the meaning of "source and origin" in mind.

4. Paul May Use Kephalē to Mean "Authority Over," But He Never Uses It In a Way That Limits or Qualifies Women's Ministry in the Public Gathering

Here's my contention. Given the ambiguity of Paul's meaning in his use of *kephalē*, it may be possible to believe he meant the word to signify "having authority over someone else." But, there's a strong case that he intended *kephalē* to mean "to be the source and origin of someone." But (and don't miss this crucial point!) what he can't have meant is that "headship" prohibits women from certain forms of public ministry. Verse 5 doesn't allow for that. Nor does he ever say that they can only do such a ministry "under the authority" of men.

Richard S. Cervin has written an excellent article titled "On the Significance of *Kephalē* ("Head"): A Study of the Abuse of One Greek Word." In that article, he shows how *kephalē* has been overused and abused. He also shows how both complementarians and egalitarians have overstated their case on the basis of their use and interpretation of *kephalē*. Cervin examines the use of *kephalē* in the Septuagint (the translation of the Hebrew OT into Greek in the third to second centuries BCE), among Greek authors (notably Plato, Plutarch, and Philo), and in the New Testament passages. He concludes that we need robust methodologies when investigating what such words mean, and we need to be very careful when we build a case using *kephalē*.[43]

Cervin also concludes that *kephalē* most likely carries connotations of authority and prominence in this passage, and *not* of source or origin. I say this to say that we all need to be very careful about the claims we make when using words like *kephalē* to build our theological case.

---

42. Bird, *Bourgeois Babes, Bossy Wives, and Bobby Haircuts*, 25.
43. Cervin, "On the Significance of Kephalē ('Head')."

But here's the thing. If you interpret *kephalē* ("head") in this passage to mean "having authority over someone," you should not miss the point that Paul *does not* use an argument from such male headship to limit the ministries women can engage in. In fact, he makes it clear that as long as believers maintain order and modesty in their shared life together, then both women and men can engage in public ministry. This is women and men doing ministry in corporate worship—that is, the public gathering of men, women, and children—not some restricted gathering for "women only."

5. Viewing Kephalē as Meaning "Having Authority Over" May Lead You Toward the Arian Heresy

Paul cannot mean that the Father is "head over" the Son (in terms of authority) just as men are "head over" women (in the same terms). As Kevin Giles has skillfully demonstrated, arguing such a case "depicts the Trinity hierarchically and this implies the Arian heresy."[44]

6. Paul Affirms Male-Female Differentiation and the Integration of Women and Their Gifts into Public Worship

In this passage, Paul is very concerned about the witness of the Corinthians before a watching world. And I think it's also obvious that he wants them to maintain appropriate cultural gender differentiations and attire, as they seek to honor the differences between women and men—gender differences purposed by God from the very beginning. Paul consistently maintains that women and men are both different and equal. Their God-given gender differentiation is important, as are their God-given gifts for the building up and edifying of the church.

Michael Bird makes the following observation, as he paraphrases Roy Ciampa and Brian Rosner: "Paul affirms three things here: (1) respect for a creation mandate to maintain and celebrate gender distinctions between the sexes; (2) a respect for culturally specific ways of guarding moral and sexual purity; and (3) a commitment to fully integrating women and their gifts into the experience of the worshipping community."[45]

44. Giles, *What the Bible Actually Teaches on Women*, 114.
45. Bird, *Bourgeois Babes, Bossy Wives, and Bobby Haircuts*, 27.

Evangelical egalitarians are clear on this key point. "*We agree this passage affirms male-female differentiation; we disagree this passage teaches the permanent subordination of women.*"[46] We also disagree that this passage limits or qualifies the public ministries that women can exercise. This affirms, instead, that this passage does the opposite: 1 Cor 11:2–16 affirms and further legitimizes the public ministries of women in the gathered assemblies of Christ's church.

1 Corinthians 14:26–40

What then shall we say, brothers and sisters? When you come together, each of you has a hymn, or a word of instruction, a revelation, a tongue or an interpretation. Everything must be done so that the church may be built up. (1 Cor 14:26)

Women should remain silent in the churches. They are not allowed to speak, but must be in submission, as the law says. If they want to inquire about something, they should ask their own husbands at home; for it is disgraceful for a woman to speak in the church. (14:34–35).

Therefore my brothers and sisters, be eager to prophesy, and do not forbid speaking in tongues. But everything should be done in a fitting and orderly way. (14:39–40)

Another challenging passage! On the one hand, Paul is encouraging women and men alike to do these things in the public assembly of believers (the "ecclesia," ἐκκλησία): bring prophecies, hymns, words of instruction (teaching), revelations, and tongues or interpretations. All this must be done in a fitting and orderly way, so that the whole church may be built up. On the other hand, Paul says women should be silent, and be in submission, and ask questions when they get home with their husbands. So, what's going on?

The most exegetically plausible explanation is "that Paul is forbidding women from asking disruptive questions in the little house-churches."[47] This explanation honors Paul's encouragement for both women and men to bring prophecies, instructions, and other contributions. It also explains why Paul is requiring women to be silent (i.e., stop interrupting), be in

46. Giles, *What the Bible Actually Teaches on Women*, 112.
47. Giles, *What the Bible Actually Teaches on Women*, 118.

submission (i.e., don't assert yourself over others, which some women in Corinth seem to have been in the habit of doing), and take their animated enquiries home (i.e., everything should be done in an orderly and fitting way). It also explains verses 27–33 and 36–40, and the emphasis on using spiritual gifts, but doing so with a focus on good order in public worship.

There is another possibility that must be taken seriously. It significantly influences how much weight we give these words, and whether we can or cannot build theologies and practices around them. And that is that 1 Cor 14:34–35 is an interpolation.

Philip Payne offers significant evidence to show that the reason why 1 Cor 14:34–35 is out of step with the rest of the passage is because it is a later addition, not in the original, and not written by Paul (Gordon Fee makes the same argument). Early manuscripts support the omission of 1 Cor 14:34–35. In early manuscripts, 1 Cor 14:34–35 is added to different places in 1 Cor 14. Furthermore, Codex Vaticanus has marks that suggest these verses are an interpolation. Payne notes the following. "Clement of Alexander reflects a text of 1 Corinthians without 1 Corinthians 14:34–35." "The Apostolic Fathers give no sign of awareness of 1 Corinthians 14:34–35." "There is high incidence of textual variants in 1 Corinthians 14:34–35."[48] And then there is internal evidence that this is an interpolation, including the ways it contradicts other parts of the chapter, the way it interrupts the flow of Paul's argument in the chapter, and so on. I haven't gone into the evidence in depth, but Payne makes a compelling case for 1 Cor 14:34–35 being a later, non-Pauline addition (interpolation). He writes,

"The thesis that 1 Cor 14:34–35 is an interpolation fits the external and the internal evidence far better than any other thesis. If 1 Cor 14:34–35 is a non-Pauline interpolation, it does not carry apostolic authority and should not be used as such to restrict the speaking ministries of women, nor should it influence the exegesis of other NT passages."[49] The exegetical and theological rule of thumb is that if a text is under suspicion—if there is evidence that it wasn't in the original manuscript—then it cannot be used to determine our theology and practice, or the way we read and apply other Bible texts.

If you reject the interpolation theory (as some scholars do), then the most likely exegetical explanation is that Paul is forbidding women from asking disruptive questions in small, intimate, house church gatherings,

48. Payne, *Man and Woman, One in Christ*, 217–67.

49. Payne, *Man and Woman, One in Christ*, 267.

and that Paul is trying to get wives to relate better to their husbands in the public gathering, and at home. Paul cannot be prohibiting women from teaching and speaking in the public assembly, because either side of 1 Cor 14:34–35 involves Paul encouraging women to speak up and use their gifts. Paul's instructions in 1 Cor 14 don't prevent women from teaching and leading in the public gathering. Instead, his instructions ensure orderliness and decorum. Marital tensions are avoided, godly submission to Christian leadership is maintained, and Christian witness and credibility is bolstered. Moreover, these instructions prevent "the church's inclusion of women in worship from being mistaken for one of the secret and orgiastic mystery cults that had reputations for feminine excesses."[50]

Ephesians 5:21–33 and Colossians 3:11–25

Submit to one another out of reverence for Christ. Wives, submit yourselves to your own husbands as you do to the Lord. For the husband is the head of the wife as Christ is the head of the church, so also wives should submit to their husbands in everything. Husbands, love your wives, just as Christ loved the church and gave himself up for her . . . (Eph 5:21–25)

Let the peace of Christ rule in your hearts, since as members of one body you were called to peace. And be thankful. Let the message of Christ dwell among you richly as you teach and admonish one another with all wisdom through psalms, hymns, and songs from the Spirit, singing to God with gratitude in your hearts. And whatever you do, whether in word or deed, do it all in the name of the Lord Jesus, giving thanks to God the Father through him. Wives, submit yourselves to your husbands, as is fitting in the Lord. Husbands, love your wives and do not be harsh with them. (Col 3:15–19)

Among other things, these two chapters contain instructions for Christian households, and guidelines for husband-wife relationships. Before we look at what they say about husband-wife relationships, we should take careful note about how Paul frames these discussions. What context does he put these discussions in?

---

50. Bird, *Bourgeois Babes, Bossy Wives, and Bobby Haircuts*, 30.

Here are a few of the relational, cultural, and theological contexts that frame Paul's instructions on husband-wife relationships. It's important that we see this context before we get into what Paul says about husbands and wives. Everything he says about husbands and wives and how they should relate to each other is shaped by these twelve Christian concerns and convictions. (1) Follow God's example, walking in the way of love, just as Christ loved us and sacrificed himself (Eph 5:1–2). (2) Put away immorality, greed, heresy, and impurity (Eph 5:3–7). (3) Live as children of light, in goodness, righteousness, and truth (Eph 5:8–14). (4) Guard your gospel-witness, be filled with the Spirit, edify each other, and be thankful to God for everything (Eph 5:15–20). (5) Practice mutual submission by "submitting to one another out of reverence for Christ" (Eph 5:21). (6) Establish godly, compassionate, loving, and Christlike households, imitating Christ (Eph 5:21–33). (7) Set your hearts on things above, and live godly and righteous lives, putting on the new self, which is being renewed by God in Christ (Col 3:1–10). (8) There's no "Gentile or Jew, circumcised or uncircumcised, barbarian, Scythian, slave or free, but Christ is all, and is in all." You are one in Christ Jesus—echoing the words of Gal 3:28 (Col 3:11). (9) Be a people of holiness, compassion, kindness, humility, gentleness, patience, forbearance, forgiveness, unity, and, above all, love (Col 3:12–14). (10) Pursue peaceful relationships with each other, build each other up in faith and love, and be thankful (Col 3:15–17). (11) Establish households that honor Christ and his gospel (Col 3:18–22). (12) Do everything out of reverence for Jesus Christ, with a passion to serve and glorify him, and with a view to your eternal inheritance (Col 3:23–25).

When I was a young pastor, I used to think that I had to come up with creative sermon outlines. How wrong I was! The most useful and striking outlines and material are always right there in the passage itself. Look at the brilliance of these two chapters, and the way Paul develops his case!

Let's start with Ephesians 5. Before Paul gets to the discussion about husbands and wives, he talks about following Christ's example of love and self-sacrifice (5:1–2), living upright and holy lives (5:3–14), guarding your gospel witness, being filled with the Spirit, edifying each other, and being thankful (5:15–20). He then frames the discussion about submission by calling for *mutual submission*: "Submit to one another out of reverence for Christ" (5:21). Paul's guidelines for husbands and wives, slaves and free, and parents and children tend to follow the cultural customs of his day, but he infuses and reimagines these customs with Christian values and virtues, including a distinct focus on mutuality and love.

Paul's instructions for husbands to love their wives "just as Christ loved the church," and for wives to submit to their husbands, must be put in the context of *mutuality*—mutual submission, mutual love, mutual compassion, mutual thankfulness, mutual gospel witness, mutual edification, and a mutual desire to honor God in everything. Among God's people, mutual submission is the norm and the rule. Hierarchies based on power and control are contrary to the gospel, and come out of a diseased social and theological imagination. The church still needs leadership, and we are to honor those who offer godly leadership in the church and the home. But that leadership must be expressed through love and a commitment to mutuality and mutual submission. Paul's call for mutuality in the church, for mutuality between men and women, and specifically for mutuality in marriage, was revolutionary and quite countercultural in the first-century Greco-Roman context. And our churches and marriages need mutuality and mutual submission today as much as they ever did!

In Eph 5:21–33 and Col 3:11–25, Paul clearly calls for women, slaves, and children to submit to husbands, masters, and parents. In turn, husbands, masters, and parents are to love, care for, and respect women, slaves, and children. The Christocentricity of these passages is striking. Christ is our model of love and self-sacrifice, and everything we do should honor Christ and his gospel, and glorify God.

But these instructions about submission aren't as straightforward to interpret as they may seem. Firstly, children and parents had very different kinds of relationships in the first century compared with our age. These first-century parent-child relationships were marked by patriarchy and also by particular, gender-based restrictions and obligations on sons and daughters. Parents made all kinds of decisions for their children (including marriage and employment) and had extraordinary authority over their adult children too, in contrast to modern cultures. These parent-child (and, note, these father-daughter relationships) don't directly parallel our culture. So, we've got to be very careful as we apply Paul's words.

Secondly, Paul tells slaves to "obey your earthly masters in everything" (Col 3:22). Such verses have been seriously abused to justify slavery and apartheid, and, today, everyone agrees that we need to interpret Paul's words in the light of their cultural context—not as a timeless instruction for slaves to accept their lot and submit to their masters, and not for people to appeal to the Bible as justification for slavery.

Thirdly, it seems clear to me that Paul tells wives to submit to their husbands. He draws a direct parallel between the headship of Christ and the church (Eph 5:22–24). That may sound jarring to egalitarian ears, but Paul doesn't retreat from his instructions on this matter. Paul's theological justifications for the relationship between husbands and wives is much more extensive than his comments about slaves-masters and children-parents. But it's interesting how he sandwiches those words to wives in Eph 5:22 between two things: (1) the call for *mutual submission* in verse 21, and (2) long instructions for *men to be loving, nurturing, and self-sacrificing* (following the example of Christ). Men must love their wives as they love themselves, and as Christ loved the church and gave himself up for her (verses 1–2, 23–33). Again, Paul tells women to submit to their husbands; but he frames this instruction in the context of mutual submission, and men practicing loving, considerate, wholehearted self-sacrifice (patterned after the ultimate self-sacrificial love expressed in Jesus Christ). Paul assumes a culture of male headship, and he assumes this will be the norm in a marriage (for Paul, unlike us, most marriages happened within patriarchal rather than egalitarian cultures). But Paul does something astonishing—he portrays this relationship in terms of mutuality and love, and self-sacrifice on the part of the husband. The man is called to love his wife utterly, as Christ loves the church, and to completely give himself to her well-being and flourishing.

Paul is writing into a culture where wives, slaves, and children (and their husbands, masters, and parents) exist within patriarchal, aristocratic, hierarchical, patron-client, honor-shame, monarchical structures. So, our interpretation of what we should do with these words about wives-husbands, slaves-masters, and children-parents isn't anywhere near as straightforward as some would claim.

Paul is moving in the direction of mutuality and equality in these verses, which isn't surprising, because that's the trajectory of Scripture. Today, even complementarian Christians would deny that we should take Paul's words about children and slaves in this passage at face value (with all the cultural background and expectations associated with Paul's words). Slavery in all forms is unacceptable and abhorrent. The relations between children and parents take different forms in different cultures ("children, obey your parents in everything," if interpreted through the lens of first-century patriarchal cultures, would prevent many adolescents converting to Christianity today). So, we also have to read his instructions to husbands and wives in their cultural context. Paul sees wives submitting to husbands as the norm in first-century culture, but he revolutionizes this arrangement by calling for mutual submission (and self-sacrificial love by men). Paul draws a parallel between wives submitting to husbands and the church submitting to Christ. But he goes on to describe how Christ gave up everything—his status, honor, position, while choosing to make himself nothing (see Phil 2)—for the sake of the church. Christ reverses our expectations of status and role! The husband becomes the loving, self-sacrificing servant of his wife, for her well-being and "radiance" (Eph 5:25–33).

If Paul is moving in the direction of mutuality and equality within the context of a patriarchal cultural reality, why wouldn't Christian marriages today *even further* explore the possibilities of mutuality and equality within the context of Western cultures that are usually egalitarian?

The type of marriage that Paul is describing is one of mutual submission, mutual love, and mutual self-sacrifice. While that's possible in a considerate complementarian marriage, in practice that marriage looks very egalitarian. I. Howard Marshall concludes: "My contention is that in the passages we have examined, when rightly understood, patriarchalism is not given a theological grounding as the only possible structure, and that the gospel itself leads us out of patriarchalism into a different kind of relationship that mirrors more adequately the mutual love and respect that is God's purpose for his redeemed people."[51]

In Ephesians 5, Paul shows us what mutual submission looks like in a marriage. This is a peaceful, thankful, nurturing, and Christ-honoring household (Col 3), characterized by love, unity, respect, and self-sacrifice (Eph 5). In a marriage where mutual submission is practiced, wives don't force their personalities or opinions on their husbands but, instead, honor them. Conversely, husbands give up power and control, and choose to sacrifice themselves and their desires for their wives, loving them fully and completely, as Christ loved the church. Both husbands and wives submit themselves to each other (and to Christ in each other) for each other's well-being and spiritual growth, and for the sake of the gospel of Jesus Christ.

51. Pierce et al., *Discovering Biblical Equality*, 204.

Titus 1:5–9; Titus 2:3–5; and 1 Timothy 3:1–13

An elder must be blameless, faithful to his wife, a man whose children believe and are not open to the charge of being wild and disobedient. (Titus 1:6)

Likewise, teach the older women to be reverent in the way they live, not to be slanderers or addicted to much wine, but to teach what is good. Then they can urge the younger women to love their husbands and children, to be self-controlled and pure, to be busy at home, to be kind, and to be subject to their husbands, so that no one will malign the word of God. (Titus 2:3–5)

Here is a trustworthy saying: Whoever aspires to be an overseer desires a noble task. Now the overseer is to be above reproach, faithful to his wife . . . He must manage his own family well and see that his children obey him, and he must do so in a manner worthy of full respect. (If anyone does not know how to manage his own family, how can he take care of God's church?) . . . In the same way, the women are to be worthy of respect, not malicious talkers but temperate and trustworthy in everything. A deacon must be faithful to his wife and must manage his children and his household well. (1 Tim 3:1–5, 11–12)

Much of what I said about Eph 5:21–33 and Col 3:11–25 could also be said of Titus 2:3–5 and 1 Tim 3:1–13. Paul is writing into a patriarchal culture, and his words must be interpreted with care. Again, no one today would support the idea that the church should teach those in modern-day slavery to be submissive and accept their lot. Paul's instructions to "Teach slaves to be subject to their masters in everything, to try to please them, not to talk back to them" (Titus 2:9) are read by the vast majority of Christians today in the light of their cultural context, and through the lens of our modern shared conviction that slavery contradicts Scripture and is an offense to God and his gospel, and is a violation of human freedom and dignity.

Paul expects wives "to be subject to their husbands" and husbands "to manage their children and households well"; as you would anticipate in the context of first-century Greco-Roman culture. As we have seen in Eph 5, these relationships must be shaped around *mutual submission* and *a shared commitment* to godliness, love, sacrifice, edification, and God's glory. In effect, *husbands and wives are submitting to each other as unto Christ*. Here Paul emphasizes that everything should be done for the sake of the gospel

(Titus 2:11–14). The trajectory in Paul and throughout the Bible is mutuality and equality, as we have already seen.

The additional question that emerges from these texts is whether women can serve as overseers and deacons. These passages do *not* prevent women from serving as overseers and deacons. We can say that emphatically. So, here I take a few moments to summarize some of the reasons why these passages allow both women and men to serve as deacons and overseers.

Let's start with the importance of getting the translation right. Many English translations incorrectly add masculine pronouns to 1 Tim 3:1–13 and Titus 1:5–9. This gives the false impression that only men can serve as overseers and deacons. But, the truth is that *there are no masculine pronouns* in these passages in the original Greek. Not a single masculine pronoun is offered, so many of the English versions of these passages can be quite misleading.

Furthermore, nothing is said in these passages (i.e., no qualifications are given) that prevents women from serving in these roles. All qualifications may equally be applied to women and men, save for the requirement for men to be monogamous.

The references to being a "one woman man" in 1 Tim 3:2, 12 and Titus 1:6 are probably dealing with the issue of polygamy and adultery. (Women didn't have multiple husbands, and it was the men who visited mistresses and prostitutes.) This "one woman man" phrase does not exclude married women from these roles, nor does it exclude single women and men.

If managing a household is a requirement for entry into these roles, then Paul and Jesus don't qualify. Nor do many of the great leaders of the church throughout its history.

Paul calls Phoebe a deacon of the church in Cenchrea, so he clearly believed that women could and should serve as deacons. In fact, the Greek word that Paul uses of Phoebe in Rom 16:1–2 (*prostatis*) means "leader" or "ruler," and could roughly be considered the equivalent of "overseer." (As an aside, it's hard to see how Priscilla and Junia didn't at least serve at the level of overseers, even if they were never called by that title. So, it seems obvious to me that Paul believed that women could and should serve at this level of leadership in the churches.)

If, as I argue, the qualifications in 1 Timothy 3 can be applied to male and female overseers and deacons, then that further explains verses 11 and

12. Paul charges male deacons/overseers to be faithful to their wives, and female deacons/overseers to be worthy of respect in every way.

Paul says anyone can aspire to be an overseer and doesn't qualify this with a reference to gender (1 Tim 3:1). "Whoever aspires" means "*whoever* aspires."

Moving beyond the texts themselves, Philip Payne notes that there are "sixty-one inscriptions and forty literary references to female deacons through the sixth century AD in the East, where the church in Ephesus was located."[52]

There is nothing in these passages that prevents women from serving as senior church leaders (including deacons, preachers, teachers, or overseers). In fact, I argue that the opposite is true. These verses encourage all people—women and men—to aspire to be an overseer, and sets out the qualifications to perform this noble role.

1 Timothy 2:8–15

> *Therefore I want the men everywhere to pray, lifting up holy hands without anger or disputing. I also want the women to dress modestly, with decency and propriety, adorning themselves, not with elaborate hairstyles or gold or pearls or expensive clothes, but with good deeds, appropriate for women who profess to worship God. A woman should learn in quietness and full submission. I do not permit a woman to teach or to assume authority over a man; she must be quiet. For Adam was formed first, then Eve. And Adam was not the one deceived; it was the woman who was deceived and became a sinner. But women will be saved through childbearing—if they continue in faith, love and holiness with propriety.* (1 Tim 2:8–15)

This is the passage used most often to restrict the ministries women can perform in the church. I think there's dangers in this passage for both complementarians (who try to restrict the ministries women can do) and for egalitarians (who try to liberate women to be able to fully lead and teach in the church). In the words of Scot McKnight, these verses are "blue parakeets." A "blue parakeet" is a Bible verse or passage that surprises, disrupts, and confronts our way of thinking. We are tempted to deny they exist. Or we ignore them. Or we make too much of them. Or we try to tame

---

52. Payne, *Man and Woman, One in Christ*, 458.

and domesticate them to our way of thinking. But God is speaking to us through them, and we must hear and respond with open hearts and minds.

I love the way Scot McKnight puts this, as he reflects on his own story:

> I have a confession. Somewhere along the line when I learned to read the Bible . . . my wide-eyed wonder of Scripture diminished and the jaw-dropping surprises were fewer and farther between. My desire to master the Bible and put it all together into my own system drained the Bible of its raw, edgy, and strange elixirs. I was caging and taming my blue parakeets . . . I now have no desire to tame blue parakeets. The Bible is what the Bible is, and I believe it. "Let the Bible be the Bible" is my motto, because teaching the Bible has taught me that the Bible will do its own work if we get out of the way and let it. Someone once said that the Bible needs no more defending than a lion, and I agree.[53]

So, let's talk for a moment about what we do with the "blue parakeets" of 1 Tim 2.

Complementarians put way too much emphasis on 1 Tim 2:9–15. Sometimes they do this without acknowledging that it's a complex and unusual passage. They selectively choose which parts of the passage to take literally ("saved through childbirth" in verse 15 is explained away, for example). They can be too quick to explain away the difficulties of interpreting and applying the whole passage. Then they build an entire theological, ecclesial, and ministry worldview and approach based on these few verses (or accept a complementarian framework offered them by their teachers). They drag in other biblical themes and texts—often unjustifiably and without due attention to their own meaning and biblical context—in order to support that predetermined theological system (or to appear not to be building a theological and ministry structure on what amounts to a few verses). The end result is that more than half the church gets excluded from many ministry roles in the life of the church. And let's be honest: it really is on the basis of a few peculiar, convoluted, and difficult verses.

Egalitarians, on the other hand, can be too quick to dismiss these verses. Too often, their attempts to explain away these verses sound shallow and unconvincing. They seem to be committed to an egalitarian position regardless of what the Bible says, and it does their convictions no favors. These efforts to explain away 1 Tim 2:9–15 can come across as feeble endeavors to do away with words they don't like. Some of the arguments they

53. McKnight, *Blue Parakeet*, 36.

make for the egalitarian position are based on tight, subtle points of interpretation (and understandably so, given the complexity of these verses).
But those egalitarian arguments are not as easily digested as the traditional
view. They may be right, but they're hard to understand if we are not reading the passage in the original Greek or if we have been told that literal
readings of the Bible are always best. Those of us who are Bible-believing
egalitarians need to do a lot better.

A friend (who happens to be a world-class biblical scholar) recently
said to me that 1 Tim 2:9–15 "is an unusual passage with some unusual
terms and oddities. So, final certainties are not to be had." I agree with
him: *final certainties are not to be had.* That's why we need to be careful not to make *too much* of this passage nor *too little.* We must commit
to wrestling with this passage as best we can. This involves listening and
discerning what the Spirit is saying to us and responding with courage and
humility. And we must interpret and apply this passage in the light of the
whole revelation of God in the Bible.

Here are a few observations about this passage, and what it might say
to us about women leading and serving in the church today.

1. Men Should Stop Grumbling and Fighting; Women Should Be Modest and Virtuous (vv. 8–10)

Paul begins by challenging the men to stop grumbling and fighting, and
getting into conflicts. They should pray, lifting up holy hands to God, pre-
sumably in worship and prayerful submission to him. Paul then instructs
the women to dress modestly and simply, and to do good deeds that honor
God. Notice the relevance of these verses today. I don't think Paul is being sexist; he's just giving good practical advice. His goal throughout this
chapter is to see God's people "live peaceful and quiet lives in all godliness and holiness" so that God may be glorified and people may be saved
(1 Tim 2:1–7). Paul is just as happy to challenge the men to godliness and
true worship as he is the women. He is a "herald and an apostle," and his
passion is for the godliness, unity, and public witness of the church.

2. "Let a Woman Learn in Quietness and in All Submission" (v. 11)

There's nothing especially unusual about this statement. Both women and
men should learn in quietness and submission to the teaching of the word

of God. Notice that Paul doesn't say "in submission to men." This is *submission to God* and *submission to the teaching of sacred Scripture*.

But why direct this instruction to "learn in quietness and full submission" at the women? Why not direct it at the men? The first reason is the threat that the church faced from persecution. The second reason is the influence of female-dominated cults. Paul was likely giving regulatory instructions with particular perils in mind.

Firstly, the church was under real threat from Roman persecution. Christian women weren't excluded from the threat. They suffered hideously during the persecution. It's no great surprise—given the exceptional and threatening circumstances—that Paul should caution Timothy against allowing women to engage in actions that might single them out for persecution under these perilous conditions. Paul isn't forbidding women to function in pastoral or teaching ministries for all time. Rather, he is giving advice regarding a particular situation of peril.

Secondly, many scholars have persuasively argued that women in Ephesus had both been emboldened by their new freedom in Christ, and also influenced by surrounding female dominated cults. They appear to have been interrupting the teaching and asserting their opinions. The cult of Artemis was influential in Ephesus. A temple was built to the goddess in Ephesus. The Ephesian Artemis was considered to be the daughter of Zeus and Leto. The Ephesians held festivals in her honor, including festive processions, elaborate rituals, and other religious celebrations. Women held a special place in her cult, and there is some debate about whether she was primarily a "mother goddess" or a "savior goddess." Archaeologists have found close to six-thousand devotional inscriptions to Artemis on the site of ancient Ephesus. In ancient Greek literature, "fully one-third of the passages referring to Ephesus or things Ephesian refer to the goddess, her sanctuary, or her cult personnel."[54]

Thirdly, Scot McKnight and others have described the gender and sexual revolution that was happening in the Roman Empire at the time. The "new Roman woman" was assertive. She was "expressing her newfound freedoms in *immodest, sexually provocative, and extravagant dress*. Rome was not terribly conservative, but these women were flouting even the limits of the Romans." The new Roman woman "was noted for *snatching*

---

54. Thomas, "At Home in the City of Artemis." See also Mowczko, "1 Timothy 2:12 In Context: Artemis of Ephesus and Her Temple."

the podium for public address and teaching." And throw into that mix "*the Artemis religious fertility cult.*"[55]

In that setting, women were likely encouraged to assert their religious and spiritual convictions, often over and against men. They dress immodestly, and they have theories about women being created first and being the origin or men (see the thrust of 1 Tim 2:9–14). Fertility is important (as the cult of Artemis declares), but what really matters is "faith, love, and holiness with propriety" (1 Tim 2:15). Paul is forbidding women to teach impudently, on their own authority, or to teach false doctrines. This is because she violates her source, man: "for the head (source) of woman is man, and the head (source) of man is Christ." Again, Paul is not forbidding women once and for all (in a universal way) from functioning in pastoral or teaching roles for all time. Rather, he is giving advice regarding specific perils facing the church in Ephesus—*the persecution from the Roman Empire and the influence of the female dominated cults in Ephesus.*

Women learning in "quietness and full submission" makes a lot of sense in that context. Paul is instructing Timothy to ensure that the women who desire to learn of the deep truths of the Christian faith must have a spirit of submission to God and to the truths of the gospel. They are to live virtuous lives characterized by good deeds. Then, they run less risk from the persecution, and stand as a contrast to the self-interested spirit of their age, so pervasive in Ephesus and its cults.

By the way, notice that Paul doesn't say "women should learn," he says, "a woman should learn." Some have made the case that he has a particular woman in mind, and Timothy knows who he's talking about. This person may have been argumentative and introducing all kinds of false teaching. It's impossible to be sure about this, because Paul doesn't name a specific person. But it's worth keeping that grammatical indication in mind.

But if you apply this verse to women in general (and don't like the idea of it being directed at one particular Ephesian woman), you should still note that Paul doesn't say that women will *always* remain in a submissive, learning posture. He says that *learning* women should be quiet and submissive. Such submission is important when you are learning. It's submission to God, the sacred Scriptures, the gospel, and the teacher. But it doesn't preclude you from one day being a teacher yourself!

55. McKnight, *Blue Parakeet*, 198–99.

3. "I Am Not Now Permitting" Isn't a Permanent or
Universal Prohibition on Women Leading and Teaching (v. 12)

Philip Payne and others have argued that "I do not permit a woman to teach" isn't the best translation of the Greek text. "I am not permitting" is a better translation.[56] "I am not permitting" suggests a present and specific instruction for a particular and time-bound problem at Ephesus (*not* a permanent or universal prohibition on women teaching).

Various scholars have shown that Paul's use of the present active indicative *epitrepō* with the negative *ouk* ("I am not permitting . . .") strongly suggests a specific instruction about a particular situation. In the vast majority of cases where *epitrepō* is used in the New Testament, and every time in the Greek Old Testament, the reference is to "a specific time or for a short or limited duration only."[57]

And when Paul says, "assuming authority over a man," he uses a peculiar word too. He uses the word *authentein*, which is used nowhere else in the Greek New Testament, and is quite different from the word that is usually used for authority: *exousia*. I don't want to make too much of this, but I think it should make us cautious as we try to understand Paul's meaning. Philip Payne says the best way to translate this sentence (in light of the context and the best lexical support) is "I am not permitting a woman to assume authority to teach a man."[58] In other words, those women (or a particular woman) who asserts a self-assumed authority over men (or a man) bring disgrace on the church and the gospel. This is especially true if they are teaching false doctrine and leading people astray. This isn't prohibiting women from ever having authority in the church or from ever being in positions of authority over men in the church. It is prohibiting self-assumed authority, especially when it involved false teaching.

4. Who Was Formed First, Who Was Deceived, and
What's With the Reference to Childbearing? (vv. 13–15)

Verses 13 and 14 are likely a reference (and refutation) of the origin stories in the cult of Artemis, preventing women from drawing on that mythology to justify certain behavior and attitudes. The new Roman women were

---

56. Payne, *Man and Woman, One in Christ*, 320.

57. Payne, *Man and Woman, One in Christ*, 320.

58. Payne, *Man and Woman, One in Christ*, 395.

most likely asserting gender order too, saying that since men are born of women then they take precedence. Men are subordinate to women in that arrangement, and the new Roman woman will make sure of it.[59]

Then we come to verse 15. A literal understanding of verse 15 would never agree with our conviction that we are saved by faith in Jesus Christ through grace alone. Women aren't saved through childbirth, but on the exact same basis as men—the saving work and person of Jesus Christ.

No one really knows what this strange verse means. Paul may be talking here of women being saved from the evils, perils, and perversities of their (Ephesian and Greco-Roman) generation, or from the current Roman persecution. Or he may be referring to the focus on fertility seen in the cult of Artemis, and be saying something like "fertility is important, but what really matters is faith, love, and holiness with propriety." Or he may be referring to the "new Roman women's avoidance of marriage while others also suggest that he is responding to the growing attraction on the part of the new Roman women to terminate their pregnancies."[60] In doing so, he may be elevating the role of mothers and the virtue of marriage. Others suggest that this is "a synecdoche referring to Jesus."[61] What Paul is *not* doing here is using the story of Eve or the female ability to bear children as a reason for limiting women's full participation in ministry and teaching. And we know that he's *not* saying all women must marry and have babies to be saved, as that contradicts what he says in many other places.

So, what do we make of all this? *This is a complex difficult passage with some unusual and odd terms and final certainties are not to be had.* All those who read and interpret this passage—egalitarian and complementarian—should acknowledge this if they are being honest. There is, however, a strong case to be made that the women in the Ephesian church (or a particular woman in the church) were self-assuming authority over men, in a dictatorial manner. Various cultural and religious forces contributed to this scenario, as I've outlined. The men may have been grumbling and upset, and conflict was emerging in the church. False teaching is an ever-present threat, as is persecution, and these are only heightened by the problems growing in the Ephesian church. Paul, therefore, offers useful instructions on worship, for this specific situation.

59. McKnight, *Blue Parakeet*, 195.

60. McKnight, *Blue Parakeet*, 196.

61. Payne, *Man and Woman, One in Christ*, 444.

I come to the conclusion that 1 Tim 2:8–15 does not forbid or prohibit women from functioning in ministerial roles such as teaching or pastoral leadership. This conclusion is supported by my examination of this passage and its cultural history. This conclusion is also sustained by my overall reading of the Bible, and by what the Bible says to us all about women in service and leadership in the church.

1 Peter 2:13—3:7

Submit yourselves for the Lord's sake to every human authority: whether to the emperor, as the supreme authority . . . Show proper respect to everyone, love the family of believers, fear God, honor the emperor. Slaves, in reverent fear of God submit yourselves to your masters, not only to those who are good and considerate, but also to those who are harsh . . . Wives, in the same way submit yourselves to your own husbands so that, if any of them do not believe the word, they may be won over without words by the behavior of their wives, when they see the purity and reverence of your lives . . . Husbands, in the same way be considerate as you live with your wives, and treat them with respect as the weaker partner and as heirs with you of the gracious gift of life, so that nothing will hinder your prayers. (1 Pet 2:13, 17–18; 3:1–2, 7)*

We move now from the writings of Paul to a passage in 1 Peter. Before we get to Peter's guidance for husbands and wives we should note the context of these verses. (1) Peter praises "the God and father of our Lord Jesus Christ" for our living hope, the "salvation of our souls" (1:1–10). (2) He exhorts God's people "scattered throughout the provinces of Pontus, Galatia, Cappadocia, Asia and Bithynia" to be "alert and sober" and live holy lives. This includes putting away sin and conflict and growing "up in your salvation" (1:13—2:3). We are living stones, chosen people, a holy nation, God's special possession, brought into God's wonderful light (2:4–10). (3) Peter exhorts the church to live godly lives in a pagan world, including submitting to governing authorities and slave masters (2:11–25). (4) Wives should submit to their husbands, and cultivate inner beauty, with the hope of winning non-believing husbands to Christ. Husbands should show their wives consideration, respect, care, and protection, since they are "heirs with you of the gracious gift of life" and "so that nothing will hinder your prayers." "Finally, all of you, be like-minded, be sympathetic, love one another, be compassionate and humble" (3:1–8). (5) If you are going to suffer in this world, then make sure it is suffering for doing good (3:8–22).

There are some expressions and instructions in these chapters that we find unusual today. All of us, regardless of our theological position, interpret them through the words of the rest of the Bible.

One example is Peter's instruction to submit yourselves to "every human authority"—emperors and governors alike. "Fear God, honor the emperor" (2:13–14, 17). We would all qualify these words, of course, and say it depends greatly on what the secular rulers are asking us to do, and who they are demanding we worship and swear allegiance to. The early Christians paid a heavy price for refusing to bow down to the emperor and the powers of the Roman Empire, and for choosing only to worship the one true God. Christians throughout the ages have taken a similar stand and paid the ultimate price as Christian martyrs.

Peter also says that slaves should submit themselves to their masters "in reverent fear of God." Slaves should submit themselves to kind and considerate masters, but also to those who are harsh. These slaves are suffering for doing good, being a good witness to the gospel, bearing under unjust suffering as they are conscious of God, and following in the footsteps of the sufferings of Christ. When Christ suffered, he trusted "him who judges justly" and did not retaliate; this is how slaves should behave too (2:18–25). We understand, of course, the sufferings of these slaves, and the terrible situation they were in. But very few people today would say this passage justifies slavery or that modern slaves should just be silent and accept their lot in life for the sake of Christ.

Just as we need to interpret Peter's words to those who are governed and enslaved, and run them through the lens of the entire Bible and their historical context; so, too, we need to interpret the words to husbands and wives. As a rule, women are physically weaker than men. But anyone who has spent any time with girls and women knows full well that they are not "the weaker sex" and they are not "the weaker partner" (3:7). The spiritual, emotional, psychological, relational, intellectual, and other strengths of women are undeniable, and easily the equal (or better!) of men. Furthermore, what do we do with domestic abuse? Should a woman submit to a husband who is violent and abusive? Today, of course, we would do everything we could to get a woman out of a violent or abusive marriage. As usual, Bible texts need careful reading and interpretation before we can apply their insights to our lives and marriages today.

Peter's advice to husbands and wives is set against the backdrop of Christians suffering under pagan Roman rule, and against the backdrop of a patriarchal society. Peter says that believers need to live godly lives at home and in the public square so that they may witness to Christ and survive the Roman oppression and persecution. For Christian women married to unbelieving men, these words are a missional (and survival) strategy for Christian life and witness in first-century pagan, patriarchal, persecuting Rome.

In *Partners in Marriage and Ministry*, Ronald W. Pierce offers examples from the lives and words of Jesus and Peter to arrive at the most sensible conclusion. "We all are urged to live at peace with others—including spouses—as much as it depends on us (compare Rom. 12:18; 1 Cor. 7:15). But, if it becomes unreasonable for conscience sake, and we have exhausted all possible options, then I believe both Jesus and Peter would say, 'Obey God over mere mortals!' (Acts 5:29)."[62]

Peter doesn't establish a timeless rule that women should always live in quiet submission to their husbands. He offers guidelines for living holy and peaceful lives, in the context of persecution, patriarchy, and unbelieving spouses. Most of us today live in very different circumstances and cultures! Peter's words do not preclude the ideal (in fact, they anticipate it). The ideal is wives and husbands living together in equality and mutuality, to the glory of God, and in reverence for Christ in each other. Such loving and mutual relationships are characterized by "inexpressible and glorious joy" (1:8), thanksgiving and holiness (1:1–25), spiritual growth (2:1–3), a sense of being chosen and special to God (2:4–10), peacefulness, godliness, freedom, and respect (2:11–25), simplicity, contentment, and growth in character (3:1–6), and prayerful, mutual consideration and respect for each other (3:1–7). What a wonderful marriage!

Peter tells wives to submit to their husbands, and to develop their character in simplicity and gentleness. But he also tells husbands to submit to their wives. Don't miss the phrase in verse 7: "Husbands, in the same way." The implied verb to "likewise" is "be submissive to." "Likewise," or "in the same way," assumes that what has been said to women also applies to men. Men should submit themselves to their wives, and do this in a spirit of consideration, respect, and prayerfulness, since their wives are mutual heirs "of the gracious gift of life." The mutuality assumed and offered in this passage is brilliant. To Christian husbands Peter says, "Husbands, in the same way submit to your wives, living with them, understanding them, and

62. Pierce, *Partners in Marriage and Ministry*, 72.

honoring them."[63] Peter and Paul follow the way of Jesus when addressing those with relational, gendered or cultural power. They say, don't dominate others, and don't hold on to power; instead, treat others as equals, with honor, dignity, respect, and love.

RECEIVING THE SPIRIT POURED OUT ON WOMEN AND MEN ALIKE—JOEL 2:28–32; ACTS 2; AND 1 CORINTHIANS 12–14

And afterward, I will pour out my Spirit on all people. Your sons and daughters will prophesy, your old men will dream dreams, your young men will see visions. Even on my servants, both men and women, I will pour out my Spirit in those days. (Joel 2:28–29)

In the last days, God says, I will pour out my Spirit on all people. Your sons and daughters will prophesy. (Acts 2:17)

There are different kinds of gifts, but the same Spirit distributes them. There are different kinds of service, but the same Lord. There are different kinds of working, but in all of them and in everyone it is the same God at work. Now to each one the manifestation of the Spirit is given for the common good . . . All these are the work of one and the same Spirit, and he distributes them to each one, just as he determines. (1 Cor 12:4–7, 11)

Writers too often skip Joel 2, Acts 2, and (the bulk of) 1 Cor 12–14 when discussing the way women can serve and lead in the church. But I think that Pentecost and the pouring out of God's gifts on both women and men is crucial to this discussion. This may be one of the reasons why Pentecostals and charismatics have often been more supportive of women in ministry than Evangelicals and Calvinists (at least in theory, if not always in practice). Those who emphasize the gifts and baptism of the Spirit may recognize more readily that "your sons and daughters will prophesy" and that God's empowering presence is available to women and men equally and alike (Joel 2 and Acts 2).

Space prevents me from going into these chapters in detail, but here I offer some brief observations. I especially focus on the implications of 1 Cor 12–14 for women and men in gathered worship. Complementarians

---

63. Pierce, *Partners in Marriage and Ministry*, 74.

can be too quick to turn to 1 Cor 14:34–35 (which we've looked at already in this book), without listening to the words or noting the important themes throughout all of 1 Cor 12–14. Paul's vision of the charismatic assembly—where *all* contribute—is shaped around Joel 2 and the Pentecostal experience of Acts 2. The Spirit is poured out on all flesh in Acts 2, and the whole people of God experience a newness like never before. Scot McKnight says, "Pentecost, so the Bible tells us, leads us to think of an *increase* in women's capacities to minister, not a decrease. Women's ministries *expand* as the Bible's plot moves forward; they do not shrink. Many today have shrunk the role of women in ministries; this flat-out contradicts the direct of the Bible's plot."[64]

What do we notice when we look at 1 Cor 12–14? How do we see the Spirit inviting and empowering both men and women for Christian ministry and service? Here are ten observations.[65]

1. Paul says that when God's people are spiritual then there are inward and outward expressions of the Holy Spirit in their lives. The Spirit fills with inspiration and grips with enthusiasm. The breath or Spirit that blows from God is usually evidenced by his transformational effect on a person's life. This transformation happens in the areas of morality, boldness in witness, passion for God, a renewed enthusiasm, and so on. The presence of the Spirit must have a noticeable impact on the life of the Christian, and consequently, on the community of believers when gathered for worship. This personal transformation and assembled impact is as equally available to women as it is to men. The Spirit baptizes and fills both women and men, and emboldens and empowers them for ministry and mission.

2. Grace is the source of all spiritual gifts. God's gifts are a free gift of grace. God is the divine Giver. Spiritual gifts are concrete expressions of God's grace. Grace is essential for all charisma and true spiritual giftedness. This must influence our understanding of the nature of all spiritual and ministry gifts. These gifts are a free gift of grace, and thus should not be a source of pride, self-exaltation, or elitism in the life of the individual Christian, nor in the assembly of believers. They are not distributed by the Spirit on the basis of gender, class, ethnicity, status, etc. God has given a variety of spiritual and

---

64. McKnight, *Blue Parakeet*, 190.

65. I first published a version of these reflections in Hill, *Salt, Light, and a City*, 248–55.

ministry gifts to both women and men according to his abundant mercy and graciousness. All credit and glory must go to him alone. The Pauline emphasis on grace-relatedness is pronounced and may not be ignored. The focus is never on gender. The focus is always on Christ, grace, and love.

Also, the nature of the word *charisma* implies numerous ways in which God's grace is evidenced in the midst of, or in the lives of, all his people. Narrow definitions or understandings of the spiritual gifts must be avoided then (say, for instance, a few ministries conducted by men). Pressure for Christians to conform to certain expressions or manifestations of the spiritual gifts must also be avoided.

Since the Pauline understanding of *charismata* is often "gifts of the Spirit," these gifts are varied, present in forms that edify the community at their point of need, and divinely originated. Diversity of expression is essential and divinely ordained. No wonder women and men express their gifts similarly and differently. The term *charisma* does not refer exclusively to a small number of supranormal gifts, but may embrace a variety of gifts including generosity and salvation itself. The term *charismata* carries overtones of grace-relatedness. However, there is also a Christ-centered undercurrent in Paul's writing when he uses this word. Ecstatic religious experiences (nor gender or competence) are not as important in the life of the Christian, and in the assembling of God's children, as expressions of giftedness (and spiritual gifts) that are permeated by grace, godly character, an ability to guard the gospel, and Christ-centeredness. God is not pleased with a form of spirituality that is individualizing, gender-focused, gender-exclusive, or self-centered. All spiritual and ministry gifts have their origin in divine grace, and serve to edify the community of believers; whether they are exercised by women or men, as the Spirit wills.

3. Various Christian groups have proposed numerous measuring sticks for determining whether the Spirit is active in the life of the believer or in the Christian community. For example, traditional Pentecostals have often proposed that speaking in tongues is evidence of the Spirit's activity in the Christian's life. Some propose gendered ways of measuring spiritual life (e.g., a gendered way of thinking about Christian spirituality can suggest that "men should be strong leaders" and "women should be soft nurturers").

Paul, however, sets the fundamental criterion of the Spirit's activity as the glorification of the Lord Jesus Christ (1 Cor 12:1–3). Women and men glorify Christ equally and alike. The holistic exaltation of Christ as Lord, that is, the testimony to this truth in every aspect of the believer's private and public life, is the primary evidence of the activity of the Spirit in the believer's life. This is also true in the assembly of Christians for public worship. This whole-of-life discipleship is how we measure spirituality and suitability for ministry. Is the person anointed by the Spirit for ministry? Are they living in holiness and grace and love? Can they guard the truth of the gospel? Are they gifted and able? Do they have good character? Those things matter, not gender.

4.   All diverse manifestations of the Spirit are for the common good. They are for building up the believing community as a whole, rather than for personal aggrandizement or exaltation. The gifts and expressions must remain secondary to their purpose (as must gender); the primary purpose is the common edification and good. Thus, when we seek to manifest the Spirit, in any noticeable and public form, we must also do some introspective searching. What are our core motivations? Is self-exaltation or personal recognition the motivation? What about ego or narcissism of some form? Or is passion for the edification of the community and desire to glorify the risen Lord the motivation? All believers must search their hearts in this matter, women and men alike.

5.   Following on from the above point, Paul's analogy of the body focuses on the edification of the community through diverse manifestations of the Spirit, as opposed to individual indulgence. These diverse manifestations are poured out by the Spirit upon women and men. Diversity in the church is essential to true unity, and to mutual edification. We need Christians to express their gifts in diverse ways—revealing the wonder of the diverse gifts, ethnicities, cultures, classes, languages, and genders in the body of Christ. The diverse manifestations of the Spirit are valuable as they contribute to the edification of the community, and the exaltation of Christ. Therefore, when the people of God gather together for public worship, conformity should not be imposed, nor diversity suppressed. Diverse manifestations of the Spirit are given by God for the maximum

edification of the body, as long as all things are done with order and godliness, and a passion for mission and witness.

The plentiful varieties of gifts are evidence of the unifying activity and presence of the Holy Spirit. Each Christian—women and men—should seek to contribute as the Spirit moves them. This is especially the case during the public gathering of the children of God for worship (a contrast to the dominant model of one person, usually male, doing most of the public teaching and ministry). The Spirit is the great equalizer. All people—from all classes, races, and both genders—are given the Spirit and his gifts for the sake of Christ and the church. Women's ministries expand as the Spirit moves on God's people.

6. Christians who function in the roles of apostle, prophet, and teacher, and indeed in any role that carries power, position, or prestige, must show humility and a willingness to recognize and honor those who serve in less visible or esteemed roles. This also carries over to the public assembling of the people of God for worship. Those members of the body who are weaker and have less esteemed gifts should not be treated with dishonor, neglect, or contempt when God's people gather together. Instead, they should be honored and allowed to give expression to their necessary and vital spiritual gifts, and natural talents.

    Women often have a tendency to serve in roles that are behind the scenes. They are team players, willing to get their hands dirty and do what it takes to serve others and make things run smoothly. I don't think I'm giving away any secrets when I say that men often prefer public roles that contain recognition. Whatever role God calls and gifts us to—public or behind the scenes—we are of great value to God and his people, as Paul's body analogy depicts. All gifts are gracious endowments of the Spirit. All gifts are equally important and given to people within the body for its mutual edification and upbuilding.

7. Love must never be set over against the gifts, for this was not Paul's point in 1 Cor 12. Rather, love is the manner in which all gifts are to function. Love transcends and embraces all spiritual and ministry gifts and acts of service. Love is the overarching source of these. The logical conclusion, therefore, is that Christians should pursue love and eagerly desire spiritual gifts. Not that Paul doesn't say "women

should desire certain gifts" and "men should desire other gifts." All are to desire "the greater gifts." But whatever role or gift we perform, we must do so with love. Christians must allow the characteristics of *agape* (divine love), as described by Paul in 1 Cor 13, to permeate every aspect of their private, public, and inner lives. This divine love must be evident in the community of believers when gathered for worship, especially in the way in which spiritual gifts function. In the community the operation of the spiritual gifts must be with patience, kindness, humility, consideration, selflessness, rejoicing with the truth, always protecting, always trusting, always hoping, always persevering.

Too often in church life, we see Christian leaders "lording it over others." These are often unaccountable, controlling, power-hungry men. But, instead, the Christian's life is to be a tangible expression of divine love. His or her use of the spiritual gifts should be evidence that such magnificent love exists, and is edifying for the whole community both in their homes and when they are gathered together to worship Christ and build each other up.

8.   In chapter 14 Paul commands the Corinthians to pursue love and eagerly desire spiritual gifts, especially the gift of prophecy. In chapter 12 he laid the foundational principle that all diverse manifestations of the Spirit are for the common good. All gifts are for building up of the community as a whole. God is able to form unity from within the context of diversity. When Christians are gathered together for public worship, therefore, spiritual gifts must not be quenched and despised.

If a woman has a gift of leadership, let her lead. If a woman has a gift of teaching, let her teach. If a woman has a gift of prophecy, let her prophesy. These gifts, given by the Spirit to both women and men, should be fanned into flame and encouraged. The criteria for these gifts isn't gender but rather character and a commitment to the gospel. And there must be godly order and respect for local church leadership, and a striving to edify, exhort, console, and instruct, and a commitment to credible public witness. Such criteria applies equally to women and men and their use of their gifts.

9.   Order must be preserved in the public assembly of believers. Paul's instructions to women and men are often culturally sensitive, because of his concern for godly order and public credibility and

witness. The general principle of "order for the sake of edification and witness" is to be applied in all situations where the people of God are gathered together, and especially for public worship. Women and men alike are responsible for cultivating lifestyles of godliness, self-control, and love. This is a life of godly orderliness, contributing to the edification of the body and its witness in the world. All things are to be done properly and in an orderly manner, for the sake of the gospel, for God is not a God of disorder, but of peace and salvation.

10. The reason why we see so many women and men involved in ministry in the early church (and throughout all ages and cultures) is because the Spirit is poured out on all flesh. Women and men are equally emboldened and empowered to serve Christ's body. Women who lead and teach enjoy the Spirit's provision, presence, protection, and power as much as men do. That is something to celebrate and affirm unreservedly. The Spirit is gender-inclusive, gifting and releasing both women and men for ministry and leadership. That's why we see so many wonderfully gifted female leaders and teachers in the worldwide church.

As Gordon Fee says, "Thus my issue in the end is not a feminist agenda—an advocacy of women in ministry. Rather, it is a Spirit agenda, a plea for the releasing of the Spirit from our strictures and structures so that the church might minister to itself and to the world more effectively."[66]

CONSIDERING THE ISSUE OF TRINITARIAN SUBORDINATION—PHILIPPIANS 2:5–11

In your relationships with one another, have the same mindset as Christ Jesus: Who, being in very nature God, did not consider equality with God something to be used to his own advantage; rather, he made himself nothing by taking the very nature of a servant, being made in human likeness. And being found in appearance as a man, he humbled himself by becoming obedient to death—even death on a cross! Therefore God exalted him to the highest place and gave him the name that is above every name, that at the name of Jesus every knee should bow, in heaven and on earth and under the earth, and

66. Pierce et al., *Discovering Biblical Equality*, 254.

every tongue acknowledge that Jesus Christ is Lord, to the glory of
God the Father. (Phil 2:5–11)

Some have used the doctrine of the Trinity to support their view on women in ministry. The subordination of women to men is compared with the eternal subordination of Christ to God. Is Christ eternally subordinate to God the Father, or are they coequal?

Most evangelical scholars today *do not* believe that the Son is eternally subordinate to the Father. The Son embraced temporary and voluntary submission and subordination during his earthly life and ministry, and during his work on the cross. Complementarians who base their theory of women's permanent subordination to men on Christ's *eternal* subordination to God are out of step with orthodox and historic Christian belief. Kevin Giles has shown this conclusively in his analysis of the writings of the church fathers, the Reformers, and the Nicene and Athanasian Creeds, in his book *The Trinity and Subordinationism.*[67] The Reformers, including Calvin, rejected the theological methods used to arrive at subordinationism. Even if such complementarians say that the Son is equal in *essence/being* but subordinate in *function/role*, they remain out of step with the widely-agreed and historic view of the Trinity (out of sync with the view of the majority of Bible-believing evangelicals). The purpose of subordinationists is often (almost always, in fact) to draw a parallel between Father/Son and men/women, and they fail miserably.

Phil 2:5–11 is an important text in this discussion. Paul depicts Christ as eternally equal with the Father, yet choosing to voluntarily and temporarily subordinate himself in the incarnation. Christ does this for the salvation of humanity, and it's *not* an eternal subordination. The final verses of the passage indicate eternal coequality with God the Father. Furthermore, the point of the passage is humility, letting go of power and status, and serving one another. "It is Christlike to willingly subordinate oneself in the service of others—and this is so for men and women . . . 'Let the same mind be in you that was in Jesus Christ.'"[68]

The subordination argument is specious, out of step with historic Christian belief, and logically flawed. It's also at odds with historic Trinitarian belief. John Jefferson Davis shows just how much so:

67. Giles, *Trinity and Subordinationism.*

68. Giles, *Trinity and Subordinationism,* 116–17.

> One wonders if the proponents of this point of view are willing to extend the logic of their arguments beyond time into eternity: If the subordination of the Son to the Father in *time* supposedly justifies the subordination of women to men in the earthly church, does the supposed subordination of the Son to the Father in eternity justify the *eternal subordination* of women to men in the heavenly church of the new creation? Are women to be *eternally* second-class citizens in the kingdom of God? Such specious arguments and misunderstandings of Scripture and tradition condemn women to positions of unending subordination and, worse still, *rob God the Son* of his coeternal and coequal glory, majesty, and lordship.[69]

Instead of entrenching divisions and power structures and hierarchies, the Trinitarian vision should lead to love, intimacy, mutuality, communion, and the full participation of all God's people. I love this quote by Leonardo Boff. "The trinitarian vision produces a vision of the church that is more communion than hierarchy, more service than power, more circular than pyramidal, more loving embrace than bending knee before authority. Such a perichoretic model of the church would submit all ecclesial functions . . . to the imperative of communion and participation by all in everything that concerns the good of all."[70]

Still, Christians should use the Trinitarian analogy cautiously and sparingly. Human nature is not like divine nature. And human relationships are not the same as those within the Godhead.

ASKING, "IS THE BIBLICAL EGALITARIAN POSITION A RECENT AND CULTURE-ACCOMMODATING INNOVATION?"

Sometimes the claim is made that biblical egalitarianism is a recent and culture-accommodating innovation. It's true that most cultures have been patriarchal and that much of the church's history has been characterized by patriarchy. It's true that religion, patriarchy, misogyny, and theology have too often gone hand-in-hand. It's true also that Christian feminism, in many of its current forms, is a recent phenomenon.

But, as I've shown in my analysis of the biblical texts, the focus of the Bible is on mutuality and equality. That's the trajectory of Scripture. As

69. Davis, "Incarnation, Trinity, and the Ordination of Women."

70. Boff, *Trinity and Society*, 153–54.

the pages of the Bible unfold, women's freedoms, dignity, and ministries increase and expand. Biblical egalitarianism is faithful to the vision and practice of Jesus and Paul. So, it's a biblically-faithful way of understanding women and men, and the roles women can perform as teachers and leaders in the church. That means it's not a recent and culture-accommodating idea—it's thousands of years old, and true to Jesus and the Bible.

The call for biblical equality and for releasing women to all forms of ministry and leadership is *not* a feminist agenda, and is *not* driven by such concerns. It is also *not* a "progressive" agenda. It *is* a biblical agenda. It *is* a Spirit agenda. It *is* a missionary agenda. It *is* a gospel agenda. It *is* a Jesus-honoring agenda, reflecting the way he welcomed and honored women. Seeing men and women as *fully equal* and equally able to participate *in all forms* of teaching, ministry, and leadership in the church is an ancient and biblical vision. It is a deeply biblical vision—and one with current and future social, missional, ethical, and ecclesial consequences for all God's people and for the world.

Biblical egalitarians do *not* advocate for sameness or a genderless society, and do *not* embrace all the concerns and perspectives of modern feminism. We do *not* discount or ignore gender or personality differences. Instead, *we call for what we see as the biblical vision*: biblical equality and the full participation of women and men in all forms of leadership, teaching, and ministry. This isn't a modern innovation—it's a biblical and, therefore, ancient and future (eschatological) vision.

Kevin Giles makes the point that the complementarian position is the novel one, and that its current form and arguments did not exist before the 1960s.[71] Giles shows how many elements of modern complementarianism are very recent and novel. Their focus on "roles" is a recent invention. The way they explain away Junia's ministry as an apostle is novel. The subordinationist use of the Trinity to talk about Father/Son and male/female relations is unprecedented and a strange theological innovation. Complementarian forms of exegesis have taken shape since the 1960s to support modern complementarian theologies and church structures. These are not historically hierarchical approaches to exegesis and biblical interpretation. Giles also shows how modern complementarians have modified their language (and exegesis) to tone down the patriarchal and misogynistic language and views of previous "traditional" generations. The complementarian position

---

71. Giles, *What the Bible Actually Teaches on Women*, 174.

and its forms of argument are novel and are *not* the "traditional" way of viewing these issues.

The question isn't "who is traditional" and "who isn't traditional"? The question is which interpretation of the Bible is most true and faithful. It's not that one party is "biblical" and that the other party isn't. The truth is that both groups are seeking to read and apply the Bible faithfully and with integrity. Once we can give each other that acknowledgment and honor, then we can move forward in fruitful conversation as we, together, examine the Bible and see what it says about women and men. And we can do this in a spirit of mutual respect, grace, honor, and love.

SUMMARIZING THE BIBLICAL CASE
FOR EQUALITY IN MINISTRY

I present a *Biblical Egalitarian Manifesto* at the end of this book. That manifesto is a clear statement of my biblical and practical convictions on equality in ministry. But I pause here to summarize what the Bible tells us about women in ministry and leadership.

Gen 1–3 proposes the full dignity and equality of women and men— a relationship marred by the fall. Gendered conflict, competition, and hierarchy are introduced through sin, and are not God's ideal for male and female relationships. The ideal in Genesis is an equal partnership of union, difference, and co-stewardship. The ideal order of creation is one of loving mutuality and equality; intimacy with God and between women and men.

In the Gospels we see Jesus showing astonishing respect for women. He included them in his ministry, welcomed them as learners (and, I argue, as aspiring teachers), and elevated their contribution and dignity. After the resurrection, Jesus made the women the "apostles to the twelve apostles." That's how Jesus honors women.

Women exercised leadership and ministry gifts throughout the Old and New Testaments. In the Old Testament, we see the examples of Miriam, Deborah, Noadiah, Huldah, Ruth, Esther, Sarah, Rebekah, Rahab, and more.

In the New Testament we have the stories of Phoebe, Priscilla, Junia, Joanna, Mary Magdalene, Susanna, and more. Phoebe, Priscilla, and Junia are striking examples of female Christian leadership in the early church. Paul speaks of many female co-laborers, including Mary, Tryphaena, Tryphosa, Persis, and others, as well as house church leaders like Lydia, Nympha,

Priscilla, and very likely Chloe. *The apostolic practice of ministry* wherever possible *matched the apostolic theology of ministry.* "The number of women in leadership in the early Pauline churches, given the cultural context, is breathtaking . . . If we consider all the early Paulines, more than one-quarter of the leaders Paul mentions by name are women, twelve in number."[72]

The Bible does not abolish the genders, nor does it minimize the differences between women and men. But verses like Gal 3:28 show that men and women are now one in Christ. Women and men are brought together as equally and completely as Jews and gentiles. All are equally honored in the family of Jesus Christ. All the barriers separating the genders and keeping women and men from being one body in love and worship and ministry are now done away with in Christ. Gal 3:28 isn't just about "spiritual status" in Christ. It has clear ecclesial implications for women, just as it does for slaves and gentiles. God welcomes *all* people into his family—regardless of ethnic, sociocultural, economic, and gender differences—and pours out his gifts on *all* people for ministry. Gal 3:28 has clear social and ecclesial implications for women.

We have looked at the small number of Pauline passages that are vigorously debated in the discussion about men and women and what roles women can perform in the church. They are challenging and important passages. Some are easier to interpret and apply than others. All must be examined in their biblical, literary, historical-cultural, and theological contexts. Then their insights and guidelines need to be carefully applied to our contemporary context. We need to look closely at the Greco-Roman culture Paul was addressing, and the relationship between the household codes and Christian witness in a pagan, patriarchal, and often persecuting society. Paul's instructions to women to submit to their husbands comes to us through a particular patriarchal cultural context. Paul offers these marital guidelines with a clear concern for how Christian women should relate to their non-believing husbands, and with attention to the difficulties presented to Christian marriage and witness by persecution and the pagan culture's accusations against Christians. We must also look at the heresies and false teachings he was addressing, and the overall theological trajectory of women and their dignity, equality, and contributions in Scripture. I think we can all agree that this is no easy task!

Some Pauline passages are strikingly egalitarian and emphasize mutuality and freedom for all to minster; while others have distinct patriarchal

---

72. Giles, *What the Bible Actually Teaches on Women*, 98.

tones. 1 Tim 2:9–15, for instance, "is an unusual passage with some unusual terms and oddities. So, *final certainties are not to be had*." But I come to the conclusion that in 1 Tim 2:8–15 Paul is offering instructions on worship for a specific situation (including false teaching and other internal and external threats to the church). "I do not permit a woman to teach" isn't the best translation of the Greek text. "I am not permitting" is a better translation, and suggests a present and specific instruction for a particular and time-bound problem at Ephesus (*not* a permanent or universal prohibition on women teaching). 1 Tim 2:9–15 does not forbid or prohibit women from functioning in ministry roles such as teaching or pastoral leadership. This conclusion is supported by an examination of this passage and its cultural history. This conclusion is also sustained by an overall reading of the Bible and what it says about women. Plus, Paul clearly empowered and released women into leadership and ministry in the churches, so he couldn't have been making a universal prohibition on women teaching and leading.

Philip Payne rightly notes that Paul's twelve "theological axioms" imply the equality of women and men in Christ. His theological convictions match his ministry practice.

In accordance with their culture, Paul and Peter do advise women to submit to their husbands. But they frame this submission in countercultural terms, with attention to equal dignity and value, and mutual submission. Both Paul and Peter emphasize mutual submission. Furthermore, Peter and Paul follow the way of Jesus when they stress those with political, religious, economic, cultural, and gendered power must not dominate others and must not hold on to power. Instead, they should treat others as equals, with honor, dignity, respect, and love, in a spirit of mutual submission and honor.

These passages on marriage relationships usually have five emphases: (1) maintaining godliness and holiness, (2) ensuring credible Christian witness, (3) glorifying God, (4) honoring and preserving the gospel, and (5) practicing mutual submission and self-sacrificial service in the way and Spirit of Jesus Christ. So let's practice and enjoy these in our marriages. And let's be husbands and wives who show the world what mutual submission, honoring our spouses, and self-sacrificial service look like. These enrich and deepen marriages. Paul and Peter emphasize mutual submission, and so should we.

At Pentecost we see the Spirit poured out on all flesh; women and men equally and alike. God's empowering presence is offered equally to women and men. The Spirit empowers women for leadership, prophecy, and teaching. These spiritual gifts, given by the Spirit to both women and men, should be fanned into flame and encouraged. The criterion for these gifts isn't gender. The criteria are character, commitment to the gospel, and openness to God's empowering and emboldening presence. The Spirit enables women and men to equally access and use their ministry and leadership gifts; to edify and build up the church, and to witness to Christ and his gospel.

We cannot use the doctrine of the Trinity as an analogy to advance the subordination of women to men. Such a proposal is out of step with historic Christianity, the views and theological methods of the Reformers (including Calvin), the biblical witness, and simple logic.

What's the picture that emerges from the Bible? It is one of men and women living and serving together in mutuality and equality in the home and the church. Women can hold any office in the church, and perform any ministry, based on their gifts and callings, not on their gender. The Pauline texts that seem to restrict women's ministries are not universal prohibitions; they are specific instructions for particular situations and contexts. The trajectory of Scripture is expanding and increasing ministry roles for women, and mutuality and equality in the home and the church. Let it be so.

3

Embracing the Practices
of Biblical Equality

In this final section, I unpack the practices of biblical equality. It's not enough to give a nod to equality. It's not enough to merely articulate a scriptural case for biblical equality. And it's not enough to give intellectual and theological assent to equality in ministry, and then do nothing about it. My friend Ian Altman recently said to me, "I think one of our real issues across our churches is that our current church cultures and systems do not allow women to naturally rise to leadership positions—boards and pastors and search committees need to take initiative and promote women to leadership roles." I think he's entirely correct. So, in this section I explore what we can do together to encourage and empower women into ministry and leadership in Christ's church.

DEALING COURAGEOUSLY WITH ISSUES
OF GENDER, JUSTICE, AND POWER
—1 PETER 5:1-11

Be shepherds of God's flock that is under your care, watching over them—not because you must, but because you are willing, as God wants you to be; not pursuing dishonest gain, but eager to serve; not lording it over those entrusted to you, but being examples to the flock. And when the Chief Shepherd appears, you will receive the crown of glory that will never fade away. In the same way, you who are younger, submit yourselves to your elders. All of you, clothe yourselves with humility toward one another, because, "God opposes the proud but

shows favor to the humble." Humble yourselves, therefore, under God's
mighty hand, that he may lift you up in due time. (1 Pet 5:2–6)

Peter's words are a good reminder that we must exercise Christian ministry
in a spirit of shepherding care, service, and humility. We must do so as
imitators and witnesses of Christ's sufferings, love, self-sacrifice, and humility. When we talk about gender issues in the church we often run into
matters of abuse, manipulation, exploitation, control, power, injustice, and
ego. These demonic spirits erode Christian faith and witness. They are not
only problems for individual leaders. They are often expressed in church
systems and structures. Peter says no, put away such things. Imitate the
Chief Shepherd. Genuinely care for people. Watch over them. Do this
gladly and willingly. Get rid of dishonest gain and manipulation and power
plays. Reject the temptations of power and control. Honor elders and protect and nurture those who are vulnerable. Clothe yourselves with humility.
Humble yourself. Be alert and sober. Resist the evils of the devil, and his
temptations to lust, greed, exploitation, and pride. The devil prowls around
like a lion waiting for someone to devour. Resist the devil's ways and stand
firm in your faith. Stand firm in the humble, nurturing, holy way of the
Chief Shepherd. Cast your anxiety on Jesus. Trust him. It's hard living this
way. You will suffer when you embrace godliness, humility, truth, and care
for others. But the God of grace will "himself restore you and make you
strong, firm and steadfast. To him be the power for ever and ever. Amen"
(1 Pet 5:10b–11).

Peter's words are timely. We see people in leadership abusing power
often. And far too often they are men in church leadership. We are all im-
pacted and implicated in patriarchy's ongoing existence. We are all impact-
ed and implicated when we allow church and organizational systems and
structures to unjustly allow some to have power and control (to their own
advantage) and others to have none (resulting in their silence, exploitation,
invisibility, and loss).

But, given the extent of sexual abuse that has emerged recently in
church and society (and given how often male church leaders have abused
women and children), I will take a few moments to speak specifically to
men. Sexual violence is so prevalent because we men are often far too
complicit. When we stay quiet about sexual harassment; we are complicit.
When we ignore everyday sexism and sexual jokes; we are complicit. When
we allow other men to treat women and girls with disrespect and disregard;
we are complicit. When we protect structures of power that keep women

silent and that keep them outside of decision making and leadership roles; we are complicit. When we allow "boy's clubs" to thrive, while excluding women and their voices and contributions and stories; we are complicit. When we know males around us are putting sexual pressure on girls and women, but we say nothing; we are complicit. When we see men using their power and position to coerce women into sexual and other intimacies and situations against their will, and yet we choose to do nothing; we are complicit. When we normalize violence, and accept or suggest that women and girls must learn to tolerate and live with the behavior of men and boys; we are complicit. When we blame the victims, and exonerate the perpetrators; we are complicit.

We need men and boys to reject toxic forms of masculinity, and ideas about manhood, and to embrace a new way: the way of humility, love, integrity, mutuality, honor, transparency, and respect. Those of us who follow Jesus Christ call this discipleship.

Men, we must choose to be held accountable. We must choose to hold each other accountable. We must choose, together, to treat women with dignity, care, honor, and respect—and to hold each other accountable for doing so. We must choose to confront other men who aren't treating women with such honor, and to challenge the structures, systems, ideas, values, and gendered roles that enable sexual violence. We must refuse to protect the structures of power (and the toxic visions of sexuality and gender) that enable women and girls to suffer violence.

When we support structures, institutions, relationships, and worldviews in which men hold all the power, and women and girls are forced to be subject to their desires; we are complicit.

Recently, in the wake of revelations about the extent of domestic violence in the churches, I offered this public apology to Christian women:

> I'm sorry for the way many Christian men have treated women in the name of faith.
>
> I'm sorry for the way these men have twisted Scripture and faith, and used these as justification to hurt and control women and families.
>
> I'm sorry that many Christian leaders haven't confronted these behaviors and the beliefs that are at the root of this violence.
>
> I'm sorry that many of us have turned a blind eye to domestic violence in our midst, or sought to excuse such violence (and our own responsibility for this suffering) when someone shines a light on it.

I'm sorry that many of us have tried to explain away our actions, and
been defensive, and made excuses.

I'm sorry and sad that we Christian leaders have sometimes behaved
in ways that have made your suffering and shame worse.

I'm sorry for the way we've often failed to listen to your experiences,
as women.

I know that apologies are only as good as the actions that follow.

I will do everything I can to listen to women and children and their
experiences, and to uphold their safety, rights, and value, and to
challenge the church and other men to do the same.[1]

The apostle Peter challenges churches and their leaders to a different
way: the way of repentance, nurture, grace, honesty, service, self-sacrifice,
love, and humility. This is another way of saying that we need to challenge
and resist the devil and his efforts to create domineering, patriarchal, abusive systems. We need to explore how this works, together.

Christian leaders and congregations need to listen to women and
minoritized and silenced persons. They give us great insight into these systems and structures. Together, we can explore how to dismantle and undo
these unjust, abusive, patriarchal systems and structures—undermining
and disrupting (and hopefully undoing) patriarchy as a system.

This includes challenging the dominant narrative that we fix these
problems through right belief and theology. Biblical belief and theology
is vital and important. We've seen that in the pages of this book. But the
powers and principalities must be resisted and confronted through our
practices and behaviors.

Will we have the courage and fortitude to take action for real change?
Protecting the flock takes action. Seeking people's well-being and nurture
and flourishing takes action. Resisting the devil takes action. Calling out
injustice and evil takes action. Standing firm takes action. Being sober and
alert takes action. Clothing yourself with humility takes action. The words
of Peter and the example of the Chief Shepherd leave us no other option.

1. Hill, "Apology to Victims of Domestic Violence in the Church."

SEEING MINISTRY AS SERVICE RATHER THAN HIERARCHY—MATTHEW 20:25–28

Jesus called them together and said, "You know that the rulers of the Gentiles lord it over them, and their high officials exercise authority over them. Not so with you. Instead, whoever wants to become great among you must be your servant, and whoever wants to be first must be your slave—just as the Son of Man did not come to be served, but to serve, and to give his life as a ransom for many. (Matt 20:25–28)

Some churches and forms of church governance are committed to maintaining hierarchical relations between men and women because they have a hierarchical vision of church and ministry. But Christian ministry is about love and service *not* power and hierarchy. Jesus calls us to reject leadership that's characterized by "exercising authority over others" (Matt 20:25–28). Jesus made this crystal clear to his disciples. And Jesus modelled this same humility, service, self-sacrifice, and submission to God in his incarnation, life, and death (Phil 2:1–8). Have the same mind as Jesus Christ. Live and serve as Jesus did. The ministry that pleases and honors God is ministry carried out in a spirit of humility and service and giving ourselves completely for the interests and well-being of others.

There is no better place to practice these commitments than in the relationships between men and women in marriage and in the church.

Jesus calls men and women to *serve each other* and *serve together* as co-laborers in the gospel, and as co-heirs of God and joint heirs with Christ (Rom 8:17).

Hierarchical and domineering leadership is unbiblical.[2] It pollutes and corrupts and erodes the church. It points away from Christ. And it degrades the church's worship and ministry and fellowship and witness. Autocratic and ego-driven leadership never brings glory to God.

In my other books I've described *servantship*—a term I prefer over servant leadership. *Servantship* is the imitation of Jesus Christ. It is imitation through love and service. *Servantship* does not dismiss notions of *leadership* or *servant leadership* altogether. But it does evaluate and reshape these concepts. It examines and reconceives notions of power and authority and influence.[3] *Servantship* cultivates a biblically informed and practi-

---

2. I first published some of the thoughts in this section on servant leadership in my book, *Globalchurch*, 353–62.

3. See the excellent treatment of servant leadership by Puerto Rican American

cal theology of leadership. This theology engages our understandings of church, servanthood, discipleship, Jesus, and mission.

Darrell Jackson is right when he says that Jesus reconceives status in the kingdom of God as bonded service.[4] Such service is "accompanied by the forfeiture of social status and personal freedom, and characterized by utter reliance on the one to whom bonded service was being rendered."[5] *Servantship* reflects the Spirit of Jesus Christ. This is especially true when *servantship* evidences the characteristics of servanthood revealed in Phil 2:1–11 and other Scriptures. The metaphor of servanthood—and the servant mission and ministry of Jesus—must shape our practices of Christian *servantship*. Only then will it be Jesus-centered and outwardly-focused Christian *servantship*.

In Phil 2:7, we read that Jesus "made himself nothing." He "emptied himself." True Christian service is movement away from selfish ambition and pride and self-centeredness. It is movement away from hierarchy and patriarchy and control. Such service is movement *toward* the same attitude as that of Jesus Christ. It's emptying oneself of pride, status, and control over others. It's being a servant. And it's humbling oneself. Self-emptied discipleship is submission to the love and will and mission of God. "The ultimate characteristic of *servantship* is love leadership. I can serve people but not love them. However, I cannot love people and not serve them. The central point of the incarnation was love."[6]

We practice and reveal *servantship* through love. And it must be the kind of love demonstrated in the incarnation and at the cross. *Servantship* isn't an abstract or idealized love. It's concrete and embodied and tangible love. Elizabeth Petersen says that we must put our theology of the cross into practice. We do this by serving the poor and broken and marginalized and silenced and oppressed. Only then can we say that we love as Jesus loved. "God is present and active *in the midst of the Broken Ones*."[7] And such loving service is costly. You cannot practice loving service without heartbreak and suffering and loss. But our eternal joy is greater.

---

theologian Efrian Agosto in *Servant Leadership: Jesus and Paul*.

4. Jackson, "For the Son of Man Did Not Come to Lead, But to Be Led," 28.

5. Jackson, "For the Son of Man Did Not Come to Lead, But to Be Led," 28.

6. Helland, "Nothing Leadership," 36. Helland coined the terms *downward missional leadership* and *nothing leadership* to describe Christian leadership.

7. Petersen and Swart, "Via the Broken Ones," 20. Italics added for emphasis.

Why do Christian leaders embrace unbiblical, self-serving, or controlling models of leadership? Why do they allow relationships to be defined by hierarchy and gender discrimination?

Sometimes they do this because of pride. And sometimes they do this because they've traded theology for pragmatics. And, often, we find ourselves immersed in patriarchal and command-and-control systems and structures.

Servantship demands biblically grounded and self-reflective theology. It thrives in an environment of theological thought and relational connection. It flourishes where God's people take Scripture seriously—including Christ's call to service and humility and love. This theological imagination is not restricted to the academy. It finds its fullest expression in a living conversation. This conversation must include scholars, leaders, churches, the gospel narrative, traditions, theologies, and cultures. It must include women and men as equals, engaged in a lifegiving and mutual exchange of hopes, experiences, and relational and biblical insights. This Christian social imagination finds its fullest expression in conversation between women and men within the needs and challenges of specific local contexts and churches.

How do we move toward *servantship*? By truly wanting to glorify Christ and not ourselves. By exalting him and making ourselves nothing. By rejecting self-seeking and self-serving and domineering forms of leadership. By embracing the servanthood exemplified by Jesus Christ. By reflecting theologically on Scripture. By meditating on passages like Philippians 2, and on the four Gospels. By putting our biblical observations and convictions into practice. And by honoring women and children as we honor men, amplifying and valuing their gifts and perspectives and experiences and contributions.

Jesus described himself as a servant. So did the apostle Paul. Repeatedly, Scripture commands us to serve Jesus and his church and his world. Jesus drives us from control to service, from competition to love, from a scarcity mind-set to a generous spirit, from pride to humility, from ambition to self-denial, from drivenness to servanthood, from ego strength to interdependent vigor, and from identification with the powerful to *servantship*. "Whoever wants to be great among you must be your servant, and whoever wants to be first must be slave of all. For even the Son of Man did not come to be served, but to serve, and to give his life as a ransom for many" (Mark 10:43–45 and Matt 20: 26–28).

Examining the biblical material, my friend Darrell Jackson forms a powerful conclusion.

> By redefining the concepts of greatness and status within the
> kingdom of God with reference to the hallmarks of service and
> humility, Jesus initiates a revolution of ruling and leadership. This
> is a vital insight for those who lead churches and Christian or-
> ganizations . . . Far from the throne-rooms and boardrooms, the
> "scum" of the earth (1 Corinthians 4:13) are exercising a ministry
> of service and humility that is frequently regarded with contempt,
> is typically accompanied by sacrificial suffering, yet which is capa-
> ble of a revolution on a cosmic scale, for it is a call to royal service
> in a kingdom against which the gates of Hades will not prevail
> (Matthew 16:18)."[8]

This biblical *servantship* is revolutionary. It redefines ruling and status
and leadership. It glorifies our Lord Jesus Christ. Through poverty, tears,
humility, righteousness, mercy, purity, peacemaking, suffering, love for
enemies, and the service of all, *servantship* witnesses to the "kingdom of
God among you" (Matt 5–7). And it joins in Jesus's mission to heal and
transform and redeem the world.

Jesus calls women and men to equally join him in his messianic mission and ministry. He pours out his Spirit on all flesh. God's empowering presence enables men and women to serve each other and to serve
together, as equals.

Those of us in Christian leadership are rarely comfortable with
service. We want to be "leaders" not "servants." So, we try to soften the
radical demands of servanthood with a hyphenated term like "servant-
leadership." That way, we can still talk about servanthood, but take on the
posture of leaders. We can wax lyrical about service, but pride ourselves
on being leaders. We can avoid the revolutionary outlook and demands
of *servantship*. Lance Ford observes, "Over the past forty years the idea
of servant leadership entered the church leadership discussion. But leaders could not bear the concept of 'servant-ship' as a stand-alone term.
'Leadership' had to be added to the equation. Being a servant is the form
of leadership urged upon us by Jesus [and] the ethos of leadership is not
a posture but a result."[9]

God calls men and women—together and as equals—to a lifestyle of
sacrifice, humility, service, and gratuitous love. Together, we reject hierarchy, patriarchy, power, and control. Instead, we seek after Spirit-empowered

8. Jackson, "For the Son of Man Did Not Come to Lead, But to Be Led," 30–31.

9. Ford, *Unleader*, 85–86.

grace, deep relationships, and genuine humility.[10] We let our theology of *servantship* emerge from our lifestyle of ministering and serving together.

As women and men we seek to serve and lead together in equal and mutual partnerships. In this way we enrich each other's ministries. We are servants, together. We serve each other, our Lord Jesus, his church, and his world. And we do this through our shared commitment to biblical equality and to mutual submission.

EMBOLDENING JUNIA'S SISTERS—ROMANS 16:7

Greet Andronicus and Junia, my fellow Jews who have been in prison with me. They are outstanding among the apostles, and they were in Christ before I was. (Rom 16:7)

It is clear that Junia was a woman (despite feeble, patriarchal, and mischievous attempts to claim otherwise). The textual and patristic evidence is overwhelming. Junia was almost certainly among those apostles (Paul, Barnabas, Silas, Apollos, Timothy, Epaphroditus, Andronicus, and Junia) who joined the original Twelve.

These apostles (*apostolos*) were "sent ones." They were church planters and missionaries who pioneered churches and spread the gospel far and wide. Andronicus and Junia are referred to as "outstanding among the apostles" (Rom 16:7). Some claim this means they were "well-known to" or "notable among" the apostles. But the Greek word *en* (ἐν) is usually translated as "among" not "to"; so the only reason you'd avoid translating this text as "among the apostles" is if you had a problem with women being apostles. Various patristics, Reformers, and other ancient biblical scholars acknowledge that Junia must have been an apostle. And the overwhelming majority of contemporary biblical scholars agree that this verse refers to Andronicus and Junia as apostles. Together, they had an outstanding reputation for their ministry.

Countless generations of pioneering missionary and church-planting Christian women have followed in the footsteps of Junia. By some estimates, over two-thirds of the world's missionaries are women. And if you spend any time with missionary women (and especially those who plant and lead churches) you quickly discover that they are involved in teaching, preaching, leading, evangelizing, planting, and often ministries of social justice and

10. Petersen and Swart, "Via the Broken Ones," 26.

action. They often have opportunities to lead and teach and pioneer that are denied them back at home. Likewise, we are increasingly seeing women break free from established patriarchal strictures and structures in the West, as they plant and pioneer churches and movements. I've lost count of the number of women I've seen graduate from seminary or theological college, look around them and see no opportunities in the established church and, therefore, venture out and plant a church, movement, or organization. Other women get a little experience in established male-dominated churches, and then take a leap of faith and pioneer successful churches and movements. Some of the most courageous, competent, and innovative pioneers I know are Christian women. Despite one or two rare male exceptions, the best preachers I've ever heard have been women. Junia's sisters are leading and expanding the local church and the church worldwide.

Imagine how the church's mission and public witness would be enhanced if we recognized, honored, resourced, and further emboldened Junia's sisters! Imagine if we caught a vision for further equipping and releasing more than half the church to advance the gospel and the reign of God in the world. This would only increase the church's credibility and the effectiveness of our mission and witness. Women face obstacles in mission and ministry. But in spite of it all—and because of their passion for Jesus and his gospel—they have advanced God's mission all over the globe and in every era and culture. It is due time we honored and emboldened Junia's sisters.

Junia and Andronicus served as pioneering apostles together. And let's also remember the shared missionary and house church leadership ministry of Priscilla and Aquila. Both couples shared a commitment to each other and to the spread of the gospel and the growth of the church. The approach of both couples to faith and mission and pioneering was mutual, shared, and, from what we can tell, equal. Sure, they were married, but they also served together as co-apostles, co-leaders, co-laborers. I think we should applaud, honor, and learn from their shared ministry spirit. Take Junia's and Andronicus's example. *Together* they were outstanding among the apostles. Together they serve as a model and example for men and women in ministry today. They show us how the gospel can be spread and the church of Jesus Christ can thrive when women and men serve together (married or otherwise), in a spirit of mutuality and equality, in mission and ministry.

It's due time we embolden Junia's sisters and affirm Andronicus's brothers, and empower them to serve together as equal partners and pioneers. Together women and men can revitalize the church and renew the world.

AMPLIFYING THE VOICES AND
HONORING THE GIFTS OF WOMEN

How do we amplify the voices and honor the gifts of women, and empower and release more female leaders in the church?

Before building a biblical case for women in ministry, Eugene Cho says these words about supporting female leadership:

> [W]e have to ask how are we as revolutionary followers of Jesus—who debunked the systemic structures during his life—working, living, ministering, writing, speaking and creating to work towards that end? Power, voice and influence are not easily pursued and obtained. It must be distributed and shared from those who have that very power, voice and influence. And because it is so counter-cultural, we have to be that much more intentional. As a male, I am embarrassed at times at the manner in which we [men] directly, indirectly, or systemically oppress our sisters.[11]

Women are held back from leadership in many areas of church and society. Their leadership credibility and credentials are constantly challenged; in ways men don't experience.

A female Christian friend recently asked me to watch a TED talk by Facebook's Chief Operating Officer, Sheryl Sanderg. It's a powerful talk on "why we have too few women leaders." The talk has been viewed almost nine million times.[12]

Sheryl Sanderg begins that talk by highlighting some concerning statistics. She shows that "women are not making it to the top of any profession anywhere in the world." Women are still kept out of the most senior roles in church and society. Sheryl shares some of the statistics below in her talk, and I add some church-related data to her points:

- Of the 190 heads of state, only nine are women.

- Globally, only 13 percent of parliamentarians are women.

---

11. Cho, "Supporting Women in All Levels of Church Leadership."
12. Sandberg, "Why We Have Too Few Women Leaders."

- In 2019 only 6.6 percent of the CEOs of Fortune 500 companies were women.

- Only 20 percent of non-profit leaders are women.

- Women face much harder choices than men, when it comes to juggling personal, family, and professional lives. Two-thirds of married male senior managers have children, whereas only one-third of married female senior managers have children.

- While the situation is slowly improving, only 10 percent of Protestant senior or solo pastors in the United States are women.[13]

- Full-time male senior pastors receive 27 percent more in pay and benefits than their female senior pastor peers.

- Pew Research examined "nine major religious organizations in the U.S. that both ordain women and allow them to hold top leadership slots. Of those organizations, four have had a woman in the top leadership position. And, so far, each of these four has had only one woman in the top position." Currently, only two of the nine major religious organizations in the United States are led by women.[14]

There's no easy fix to this problem, since we're talking about a problem that grew over many generations and that is entrenched in patriarchal systems. But we can make some changes that will help us head in the right direction.

It begins with recognizing that we have a problem. Then we need to ask ourselves some tough questions, and be prepared for the answers and be willing to change:

What are the messages we tell ourselves, the women who work among us, and our daughters? What barriers have we erected that prevent their advancement and contribution? How can we truly amplify the voices of women and honor their gifts? How are we enabling women "to sit at the table," by seeking out female friends, by listening to women, by honoring "ordinary" women, by examining our beliefs and practices, by embracing reciprocal mentoring, by praying with women, and by profiling and promoting female speakers, board members, academics, and senior leaders?

---

13. See the statistics here: https://www.christianitytoday.com/women-leaders/2015/october/state-of-female-pastors.html.

14. See the Pew Research data here: http://www.pewresearch.org/fact-tank/2016/03/02/women-relatively-rare-in-top-positions-of-religious-leadership/.

Gordon Fee writes,

> It seems a sad commentary on the church and on its understanding of the Holy Spirit that 'official' leadership and ministry is allowed to come from only one half of the community of faith. The New Testament evidence is that the Holy Spirit is gender inclusive, gifting both men and women, and thus potentially setting the whole body free for all the parts to minister and in various ways to give leadership to the others.[15]

What can we do to empower and release more female leaders? And what can we do to amplify the voices and honor the gifts of women? Here are fifteen things.

1. *Get real about empowering female leaders*

    Too often, we give a "nod" to women in ministry and leadership but do nothing to bring about change. It's one thing to limit women's ministry because of biblical convictions; it's a shameful thing to say you're egalitarian (or all in favor of women in leadership) and then do nothing to make that a reality. We need to move beyond giving "a nod" to females in leadership, and actually prioritize this and do something about it now.

2. *Enable women to sit at the table*

    Most Christian organizations and churches don't enable women to sit at the table. Sheryl Sanderg says that we need to add something to this: women often systematically underestimate their own abilities. Women don't negotiate for themselves in the church and the workforce. Men attribute their success to themselves and their abilities, while women attribute their success to other external factors (not to themselves).

    We need to create space for women to sit at the table. Just like men, women need spaces where they can contribute and learn and grow. No one becomes a brilliant leader overnight. We all need support, permission, and mentoring. We all need to take risks, make mistakes, and grow into leadership.

    So, just like men, women need people who believe in them and help them believe in themselves. Sheryl Sanderg provides a role model for this. She says to women: "Believe you've got the A. Reach

15. Pierce et al., *Discovering Biblical Equality*, 254.

for the promotion. Ignore the inner voices. Know you'll pay the price for assertiveness but keep your hand up and your voice up anyway."[16]

Those of us who are senior leaders in Christian organizations need to see that men are reaching for opportunities more than women, and choose to help women reach for those opportunities. Decide to push women forward into leadership, honor their gifts and talents, and encourage them to believe in themselves and have a go. Address the systems and structures that prevent female leadership, and enable women to "sit at the leadership table."

So, what can we do? Make sure women are at the leadership table in our churches and teams and boards (especially in leadership roles and on boards). Encourage women to be assertive and to believe in themselves. Don't be satisfied until you've got many women on your ministry team and your board. Encourage women to reach for promotions and recognitions. Find ways to coach and mentor women into senior roles (this won't happen without intentionality).

3.   *Help women see women at the table*

It's really hard to believe you can do something if you don't have role models. So, we need to help women see other women at the table. This involves promoting women into senior leadership positions. (By the way, if you think that's tokenism, you haven't been paying attention to the talented women all around you!). Invite females in key leadership positions within the church and the workforce to undertake training and development for teams, and to share their stories. Provide "networking" opportunities for women, so that they can learn from women leaders who have gone before them.

4.   *Transform male-dominated cultures*

The church is one of the most male-dominated organizations on the face of the earth. Male-dominated and/or patriarchal organizational cultures are everywhere in the church.

So, we need to address and change this culture. What are the existing attitudes towards women in the church and family, and how do we shape healthier and more honoring attitudes towards women? What gets rewarded or penalized in male-dominated cultures, and how do we change that? What is our church's or organization's leadership model, and how does it reward men and restrict women?

16. Sandberg, "Why We Have Too Few Women Leaders."

Sometimes women can feel pressure to conform to the male leadership models . . . What are the alternatives to this?

We need to examine our recruitment practices and our leadership development processes. People often "recruit in their own image/gender" and "develop leaders in their own image/gender." If we have mostly men in middle and senior management or church leadership positions, it can be difficult for women to be seen as appropriate potential leaders. We need to be thorough when recruiting and ensure that selection criteria is not subtly aimed more at men. We need to invite women into our leadership training and development programs; asking women to help us reshape them so that they are accessible and relevant to both women and men.

Organizational cultures don't fix themselves. And they resist change. Transforming male-dominated organizational and leadership cultures takes courage and hard work, but it's worth it.

5. *Model and esteem real professional and personal partnerships*

Sheryl Sandberg emphasizes this in her talk, and it's highly relevant for Christian marriages and gender relationships. We need to model and esteem real partnerships between women and men—both professional partnerships in the workforce and church, *and* personal partnerships in friendships and marriage.

Research suggests that we've made more progress on this front in the workforce than in the home. Women still carry the weight of the family and housework. Women often work and do the bulk of the chores and child-rearing. But, households with equal responsibility have lower divorce rates, and much happier marriages. Plus, they honor and esteem real partnership.

So, how do we address this? We need to emphasize the importance of real partnerships between men and women in all spheres of life, including church, professions, and in the home. We must emphasize this by example, and also verbally in business meetings and social gatherings. We must take every opportunity to elevate and model equal partnerships between women and men (including emphasizing this in school and college classes, and in a multitude of church and home settings, so that younger generations of men get the message). Finally, we must encourage girls and women to settle for nothing less than real partnerships.

6. *Build cultures where women and men can equally succeed*

The church needs to make a commitment to build an environment where women and men can equally succeed. This involves addressing misogyny and sexism and patriarchy. It means settling for nothing less than equality and honor for all people—all women and all men. It means addressing subtle and unrecognized prejudices and barriers, and showing the world what redeemed and restored gender and personal relationships truly look like.

We need to find ways to encourage and coach women to stay proactive and engaged and reaching for more, at every stage in their ministries and careers. Again, Sheryl Sandberg suggests that this involves encouraging women to refuse to lean back from opportunities and leadership in anticipation of future life stages and commitments (e.g., parenting). She says encourage women to "keep your foot on the gas pedal until the very day you need to leave to have a child" (and, if you're an employer, support parental leave, and offer real opportunities to return to work, if that's what the man or woman chooses to do). Make it easier for women (and men) to return to the workforce after having children, and to continue in their career and ministry aspirations.

What else can we do? Get older women to encourage younger women to embrace this perspective. Get older men to show younger men what truly honoring and promoting women looks like, and to encourage younger men to do the same. Seek to build a culture where men and women are equally able to succeed, and equally able to be liked and respected for their accomplishments and gifts.

The challenge will be getting really practical in how we encourage women to be assertive, more confident, and reach for promotions and opportunities. But the challenge is also in addressing the hidden prejudices and barriers and sexism—and the patriarchal cultures—and addressing the cultural and leadership dynamics that prevent women from succeeding and thriving. We need Christian leaders who value this, and who can release those values into their marriages, families, churches, teams, businesses, and organizations.

7. *Stop talking and start listening*

Again, if you're a man, stop talking and start listening to women. What are they saying to you, and to your behavior, attitudes, church, and postures? Listen to the voices and concerns of women. How do they feel about what's been going on? How have they experienced marginalization, neglect, and discrimination? What visions do they have for the healing and transformation of families, churches, and societies? What leadership gifts do they have, which they're yearning to use?

8. *Honor all women*

Honor, listen to, and celebrate all women. Sometimes we honor and profile only a certain kind of strong or forceful woman. But what about the voices of other women in our churches; those who are quieter and work behind the scenes, for instance? What is God saying to us through those voices? How can we get better at listening and learning from them and honoring them?

9. *Examine your beliefs and practices*

Ask questions about how you are using Scripture and religious traditions. Examine your beliefs and practices. Are these limiting women's rights, views, and ability to lead? Or are these honoring and valuing and elevating women—inviting them to the table as equals who are fully able to use all the gifts and abilities that God has given them?

10. *Embrace reciprocal mentoring*

Embrace "reciprocal mentoring." I think that male leaders should often be paired with established and emerging female leaders, in a relationship of reciprocal mentoring. The goals are to learn from each other, to break down unconscious bias, to enrich churches and organizations, and to flip our traditional ideas of mentoring on their head.

11. *Get proactive about women speakers*

Ensure that women are speaking at your church services and at your events. Develop, profile, and listen to female speakers. If you are able, help women by making introductions to conference organizers, once or twice a year. Don't just make sure that women are involved in speaking at conferences and panels—also ensure they are planning those events. Make sure they are serving in positions of power, and have equal access to attending the conference and building dynamic networks. Get proactive. Look for female speakers at seminaries and local churches, and make a commitment to having them speak at your church, college, or event. Without a real commitment, and measurable goals, no change will happen.

12. *Ask what you're willing to give up (and gain)*

If you're a male pastor, preacher, or conference speaker, it's time to process whether or not you are willing to make the sacrifice of losing/sharing your spot for the sake of the church hearing a female voice (there's always a danger when such change begins, that we indulge in self protectionism). If you're a male pastor, it's time to speak at your church less, and encourage women to speak more. The church is much richer for that. If you're a male conference speaker, you might also take a stand and say that you won't be on a panel or speak at a conference unless women are also on the panel and speaking.

13. *Profile female Christian leaders*

Talk about female Christian leaders. Ensure that your congregation, family, and college class learn about the stories of contemporary and historical female leaders. Read books written by women. Listen to talks delivered by women. Look for histories that elevate women. Profile the stories of women in leadership, and of women pursing discipleship and faith in everyday life.

14. *Pray with women*

We are close to the people we pray with. We hear each other when we pray with each other with an open and attentive heart. Have you ever noticed that if you listen deeply to someone's prayers, you hear their desires, fears, viewpoint, hopes, and more? When we pray with others we invite them—and the Spirit in them—to speak into our lives and point us to Jesus.

15. *Make honoring women and girls a lifestyle and an institutional value*

Befriend her.

Listen to her.

Learn from her.

Honor her.

Mentor with her.

Refuse tokenism with her.

Promote her.

Appoint her.

Resource her.

Ask her.

Apologize to her.

Sponsor her.

Smash patriarchy with her.

Recognize her.

Choose equality with her.

Submit to her.

Make room for her.

Invite her.

Serve with her.

Celebrate her accomplishments with her.

Share your platform with her.

Give things up for her.

Make space for her.

Name the principalities and powers with her.

Profile her.

Quote her.

Hire her.

Stand up for her.

Pay her.

Publicly affirm her.

Preach Christ with her.

Seek justice with her.

Pray with her.

Celebrate her.

Encourage her.

Respect her.

Submit to Christ in her.[17]

The words of N. T. Wright ring true: "Just as I think we need radically to change our traditional pictures of the afterlife, away from the mediaeval models and back to the biblical ones, so we need radically to change our traditional pictures both of what men and women are and how they relate to one another within the church and indeed of what the Bible says on this

---

17. See these blog posts: Elizabeth Graham to *The Junia Project*, 2018, <https://juniaproject.com/advocate-for-women-in-ministry/>; Graham Joseph Hill to *The Global Church Project*, 2017, <https://theglobalchurchproject.com/9-ways-amplify-voices-honor-gifts-women/>; Graham Joseph Hill to *The Global Church Project*, 2018, <https://theglobalchurchproject.com/empower-female-leaders/>.

subject . . . Perhaps in our generation we have an opportunity to take a large step back in the right direction."[18]

In this book I have outlined the biblical case for equality between women and men. I have also examined scriptural passages and themes to present a biblical vision for women in ministry and leadership. The trajectory of Scripture is clear. As the pages of the Bible unfold the opportunities for women expand. As the biblical story progresses, women are empowered and emboldened for full ministry participation in the churches and equal missionary opportunities in the world.

Jesus freed and honored women. The Spirit empowers and gifts women. The Father lovingly creates and dignifies women. The Father, Son, and Holy Spirit invite women and men into equal intimacy with the Godhead and with each other. The weight and trajectory of Scripture supports equality for women and their full participation in all forms of service and ministry. Tragically, the church and its leaders have not always treated women with honor. We see too many instances in the history of the church where women have been sexually abused, oppressed, and exploited. Women have also often been denied the opportunity to make an equal and honored contribution through their passions and gifts. But, this very day, Jesus calls his local and global church to choose a different way. Jesus calls his church to honor, liberate, and affirm women, as equal and valued members of the body of Christ. Women and men can both enjoy full equality, mutual submission, and unfettered ministry in the life of the church and out in the world.

The Bible affirms women teaching, pioneering, serving, prophesying, witnessing, discipling, and leading. All the ministries that are available to men are equally available to women. Relationships between men and women must always be characterized by reciprocal honor and mutual submission. This biblical vision transforms not only our personal lives, but also our churches, neighborhood, families, and world. The church's integrity, holiness, credibility, and witness are only enhanced through the practice of biblical equality.

"Women hold up half the sky" and they make up more than half the church. It's due time that the church of Jesus Christ pursued the biblical vision of gender equality and mutual submission, and empowered both men and women in ministry.

18. Wright, "Women's Service in the Church."

Conclusion

A PRAYER

Our Father in heaven,
    revered be your name.
Our hearts long for the day when
    "Your kingdom comes,
        Your will is done,
        on earth as it is in heaven."
Show us your purpose and will,
    lead us into love and restored relationships,
    show us your grace and truth.
Free us from fear and prejudice,
    pride and insecurity,
    and striving for power and control.
Set the world right,
    restoring justice,
    healing broken relationships,
    removing divisions,
    replacing conflict with reconciliation,
    bringing peace and love between women and men,
    making us all equal,
    uniting us in a common relationship with Jesus Christ,
    forming us into Christ's family.
Forgive us for holding women back
    from using their gifts fully and freely.
Give us passion and resolve to see this change.
We are sorry
    for limiting women's freedoms,

for ignoring their gifts,
    for silencing their voices,
    for patriarchy and the abuse of power,
    for the way women have been treated in the name of faith,
    for the ways some have twisted the Bible to wound and control.
We give thanks
    for women who have persisted and spoken out,
    for women and men who have confronted patriarchy,
        abuse, and violence,
    for those who refuse to turn a blind eye,
    for those who shine a light in the darkness,
    for those who call for justice,
    for those who reject defensiveness and excuses,
    for those who listen to women's voices and respond,
    for those who accept nothing less
        than gender equality and mutual submission.
Give us courage to build churches
    that value women and girls,
    that honor women and men equally and fully,
    that practice mutual submission,
    that invite women to the table as equals,
    that enable everyone to use all their gifts fully.
Give us your empowering presence
    to confront the powers and principalities,
    to model equality and mutuality,
    to let justice roll,
    to welcome and embrace difference,
    to listen to women and children,
    to uphold their safety, rights, and value,
    to challenge the church and all men to do the same.
You have shown us what is good
    and what you require of us:
        to seek and do justice,
        to love mercy and kindness,
        to walk humbly with our God.
Shape us into one unified people,

Who are no longer separated
> by race, politics, class, or gender.

Who are one new humanity
> in Jesus Christ our Lord.

We commit to doing all we can
> to honor, elevate, value, celebrate, listen to, and respect women.

We make a steadfast commitment
> to invite women to the table,
> as equal partners in faith and leadership and life,
> and to practice and promote biblical equality.

Yours is the kingdom,
> the power and the glory,
> forever.

Amen.

Afterword
Lynn H. Cohick

Graham Joseph Hill constructs a strong case for encouraging and equipping women to serve as leaders and teachers for the whole church. He is acutely aware of the emotional toll that current systems of disenfranchisement take in women's lives. He understands that our churches are weaker and poorer when we sideline over half its members. Reading Scripture with an appreciation for its literary and historical-cultural contexts, Hill highlights the early church's critique of the sexism rooted in the ancient Greco-Roman culture. He rightly challenges the myth that recent feminist concerns create the conversation about women in ministry. It was his own exploration of the Bible, specifically Paul's example of "releasing women to serve and lead," which convinced him that he should facilitate women in leadership within the church.

If we implemented Hill's vision, what might the church look like in a decade or two? Overall, the church would be better aligned with the values of God's kingdom. I suggest at least three areas where a church that followed Hill's prescriptions would influence our needy world that is starving for the good news of the gospel. The local church would model best practices for women in the workplace and family, would highlight the beauty of God's creation including humans as male and female, and would offer a better vision for masculinity that embraces Jesus's own example.

First, local churches would set the pace for healthy work environments for women, and offer wholesome examples for family life. Healthy body image and self-esteem would grow as women embrace themselves as first and foremost a disciple "in Christ." Young women benefit from watching female role models in key leadership and decision-making roles within the church. Young men gain an appreciation for women's capabilities as they see women alongside men making decisions that impact the church and home. Hill promotes "servantship," which "drives us from control to service, from competition to love." Churches' encouragement of women's pursuit of their giftings allows women to shepherd the church theologically, financially and administratively, and to have quality mentoring experiences alongside their male counterparts. This models the creation mandate that male and female together care for God's good world (Gen 1:26–31).

Second, Hill's discussion reinforces the importance of biological sex in God's creation. Hill emphasizes that male and female are different, and explores what those differences should mean in our daily lives. Today some in the wider culture, in an effort to diminish gender disparities, deny any differences between male and female. Hill rightly rejects this approach, and instead focuses on how the differences between male and female need not lead to inequality and bias. Part of his argument focuses on the Holy Spirit gifting men and women equally to serve the whole church. Hill appropriately repudiates any argument for women's subordinate roles based on a (false) theory of the eternal subordination of the Son to the Father (see also John 5:26). In so doing, Hill encourages further exploration into the theological importance of Christ's ascension and believers' future bodily resurrection. A woman's body *qua* female will be raised immortal and perfect; how should the church affirm this reality today? As one example, the conviction that female bodies will be raised encourages churches to listen to a woman's voice and see her physical presence before the congregation. Such would counteract the current practice wherein some male pastors quote women authors in their sermons, but do not allow those same female authors to speak from the pulpit.

Third, Hill lays the groundwork for further work on masculinity. Often the "women's issue" is discussed apart from any conversation about what it means to be a man. But it is precisely that issue—the definition of masculinity—which drives so much of the debate about whether women can lead or teach men. Hill's work offers a solid foundation for women serving alongside men in all areas of the church, as equal partners. On this foundation we can build a biblical view of masculinity that follows the example of Christ Jesus.

Why do we need a new vision of masculinity? Because our picture of what it means to be a "real man" is often far from the scriptural ideal. Instead, it is closer to the wider culture's understanding, which is rooted in an Aristotelian worldview, that sees men and women as opposites, with men superior in intellect and leadership. The church follows the Aristotelian view in imagining males as inherently assertive and active, with females painted as "naturally" passive and nurturing. But as Hill points out, the biblical text does not support the binary opposition between male and female, nor the assessment that females inherently lack the qualities that make for good leadership and teaching. The early church challenged a central conviction of its day, namely that being a man meant being in charge of oneself and others. This belief manifested itself by seeking control at all costs, even committing suicide rather than face dishonor or torture. But the early church held up the martyr as the model disciple. This man or woman gave up control and courageously faced a horrific death. The Roman society saw male martyrs as effeminate, but the church viewed them as following Christ's own example of giving God control, and hoping fully in the resurrection of the body. Jesus accepted the shame of his trial, and the ignoble death on the cross. He bids all disciples, men and women, to take up their cross and follow after their crucified, risen, and ascended Lord. Christ beckons men not to strive to maintain and defend their power, but rather to embody a posture of selflessness and sacrifice.

Hill's call for change will require much heavy lifting as men release control and actively listen to women. Churches must work tirelessly to create an environment that allows men and women to thrive in their giftings. The goal is worth it: a revitalized church that is able to meet the wider world with the healing, hopeful message of the gospel.

LYNN H. COHICK
Provost/Dean and Professor of New Testament
Denver Seminary
Littleton, Colorado

Appendix:
A Biblical Egalitarian Manifesto

This *Biblical Egalitarian Manifesto* is my personal affirmation of what I believe the Bible teaches about men and women in Christ. It is my declaration about what the Bible says about gender equality in ministry. I believe the Bible teaches biblical equality, mutual submission, complementarity without hierarchy, and full participation of women and men in all areas of service and leadership in the church. It is my belief that this *Manifesto* reclaims and articulates the biblical vision for men and women in Jesus Christ.

1. All conversations about men and women in Christ should be conducted in a spirit of worship, renewed minds, discernment, self-sacrifice, humility, unity, mutual honor, peace, mutual respect, love, spiritual zeal, generosity, hospitality, reconciliation, forgiveness, and harmony (Rom 11:33—12:21).

2. All Christians should have the opportunity to wrestle with the various positions on women in ministry, so that they might arrive at their own conclusions, even if these differ from ours (Acts 17:11).

3. Men and women should have the chance to examine the relevant biblical texts and cultural issues together, and these conversations should be characterized by compassion, truthfulness, integrity, love, unity, humility, self-sacrifice, and looking to the interests of others (Phil 2:1–11).

4. Discussions about men and women in ministry must not involve false allegations or misleading rhetoric, which hurt Christian unity and spiritual maturity (1 Pet 2:1–2).

5. Biblical egalitarianism holds a high view of Scripture and its inspiration and authority. The Bible plumbs, measures, illuminates, adjudicates, enlivens, inspires, norms, instructs, and more. It guides us toward the living Word, Jesus Christ. The Bible is the authoritative

word of God, inspired by the Holy Spirit. The Bible has absolute and final authority in all aspects of corporate and individual faith, ethics, conduct, witness, and theology. Our understanding of men and women must be biblical. Biblical egalitarianism does not shy away from biblical authority—it embraces it (2 Tim 3:16–17).

6. Genesis 1–3 proposes the full dignity and equality of women and men—a beautiful, equal partnership, characterized by unity, difference, love, co-stewardship, and intimacy with God and each other. Hierarchy and conflict only emerge as a result of the fall and are not God's ideal for male-female relationships. Christians must acknowledge and celebrate the fact that the God-given creation ideal is equality, mutual stewardship, and love (Gen 1–3).

7. Men and women are equally made in God's image. God made us male and female, in his image, and for his glory (Gen 1:26–28).

8. The Bible upholds the created order throughout the Old and New Testaments. The Bible does not argue for a genderless church where women and men are undifferentiated. The biblical vision is that women and men are equal but different. The Bible *does not* teach that men and women are the same. But it *does* teach equality, complementarity, mutual submission, and oneness in Christ. Gender complementarity is ideal; but gender hierarchy is unbiblical and damaging to the whole church. I am a *non-hierarchical complementarian* who supports *gender equality* and *full access to all ministry roles for women* and men, because I believe that is the will and design of God revealed in the Bible (Gen 1:27; 2:18–25).

9. Genesis isn't the full story. As Christians, we are all a part of the new creation. Women and men equally enjoy the renewal and blessing and hope and life that comes with being a part of the new creation in Jesus Christ (2 Cor 5:14–19; Gal 6:12–16; Eph 2:11–22; 4:17–24; Col 3:1–11).

10. The Old Testament contains stories of many women who functioned in positions of leadership and responsibility. This pattern of God anointing women to lead is repeated in the New Testament, the early churches, and the churches throughout all ages. Old Testament female leaders included Miriam, Deborah, Noadiah, Huldah, Ruth, Esther, Sarah, Rebekah, and Rahab. Among them are spiritual leaders, prophets, judges, and more. The entire Scriptures show that God

takes delight in seeing women function in ministry and leadership among his people (Mic 6:4; Exod 15:20–21; Judg 4:4–6; Neh 6:14; 2 Kgs 22:8–20; 2 Chr 34:19–28).

11. Jesus honored and welcomed women into ministry, and so must his church. He invited them to carry his message and vision, to enjoy robust theological conversations, and to learn equally among men. Jesus commissioned women to evangelize among their people groups, to assume prophetic roles, and to join with him in his mission. He honored and welcomed women fully. He welcomed women to "sit at his feet" with the intention of teaching the words and message of their Teacher. Jesus made women the "apostles to the twelve apostles." The church must imitate and follow the way Jesus honored and liberated women (Mark 14; Luke 10 and 24; John 4).

12. Pentecost was a defining moment for women and men. Jesus pours out his Spirit and his spiritual gifts on women and men equally. Women and men are equally emboldened and empowered to serve Christ's body. Women who lead and teach enjoy the Spirit's provision, presence, protection, and power as much as men do. The Spirit of Christ gives gifts for ministry and mission without regard for gender. The Spirit is gender inclusive, gifting and releasing both women and men for ministry and leadership (Joel 2:28–32; Acts 2; Rom 12:6–8; 1 Cor 12–14; Eph 4:11–12; Heb 2:4; 1 Pet 4:9–11).

13. Both women and men can equally be conformed to the image of Jesus Christ. This is the goal for all disciples, regardless of gender. Jesus is equally the Lord, Savior, Teacher, Master, role model, and example for men and women (Rom 8:29; Gal 3:26–28).

14. Men and women are equally children of God through faith in Jesus Christ. We have received the spirit of adoption as sons and daughters, and are co-heirs of God and fellow heirs with Christ. Both genders enjoy all the rights, privileges, obligations, freedoms, honor, and blessings of being God's children, including being co-heirs of the kingdom of God with Jesus Christ. Men and women have equal status before God, and are equally valued, loved, and dignified (Rom 8:14–17; 2 Cor 5:16–17; Gal 3:26–28).

15. A faithful interpretation of the Bible shows that equality between men and women is God's ideal. When interpreted faithfully, the biblical instructions to husbands and wives always push in the direction

of equality and mutual submission. We must choose to reach for that ideal equality, and practice it in our marriages and ministries (Gen 1:26–28; 2:20–23; 5:1–2; 21:12; Matt 20:25–28; 23:8–9; 28:10; Mark 10:42–45; John 1:12–13; 13:13–17; Acts 1:14; 2:17–18; 18:26; 21:9; Rom 8:14–17; 16:1–7, 12–13, 15; Phil 4:2–3; Col 4:15; 1 Cor 7:3–5; 11:11–12; 12:4–11; 2 Cor 3:18; 5:16–17; Gal 3:26–28; Eph 5:21–33; 1 Pet 2:9–10; 4:10–11; 2 John 1:1–13; Rev 1:6; 5:9–10).

16. Paul the apostle's teachings on men and women in marriage and ministry must be examined in their biblical, literary, and historical-cultural contexts. Only then can they be applied to our contemporary settings. At all times we should examine their cultural context and the Christian values that undergird the instructions (glorifying God, ensuring credible witness, preserving the gospel, loving God and neighbor, and so on). This applies to Paul's instructions on ministry as well as the household codes (Eph 5:22—6:9; Col 3:18—4:1; 1 Tim 2:9–15; Titus 2:2–10; 1 Pet 2:13—3:7).

17. The Bible has a service-focused and charismatic view of leadership and ministry. All ministry is an act of service in the imitation of our Servant Lord. And all ministry flows from God's empowering presence, as he distributes his gifts to whomever he chooses, women and men equally and alike. Ministry flows from quality of character and the gifts given, not from gender. To each a ministry is given—men and women equally (Acts 2:17–18; Rom 12:3–8; 1 Cor 12:7–11; Eph 4:7; 1 Pet 4:10–11)!

18. Paul made a practice of honoring and releasing women to serve, teach, prophesy, evangelize, and lead, and so must the church today. Paul's practice of releasing women to teach and lead matched his theology of ministry. The list of women in ministry is so long in Paul's writing, that his affirmation of female leaders is undeniable. There were women prophets (Luke 2:36; Acts 2:17; 21:9; 1 Cor 11:5), women deacons (Rom 16:1), women house church leaders (Col 4:15), and husband and wife leadership teams (Acts 18:24–28; Rom 16:7). Fully one-quarter of the leaders Paul mentions by name are women (twelve in number) (Acts 18:24–28; Rom 16:1–12; 1 Cor 1:11; 11:5; 12:28; Phil 4:2–3; Col 4:15; 1 Tim 2:9).

19. Phoebe, Priscilla, and Junia are examples of first-century Christian women in senior leadership roles. In these women we see female

leaders exercising apostolic, pioneering, missionary, church planting, pastoring, teaching, and leadership gifts. Paul mentions many other female leaders in the early church. These first-century women model leadership for future generations of Christian women (Rom 16:1–7).

20. Paul's theological convictions imply the equality of women and men in Christ. They also indicate that women can serve and lead as equally and fully as men. These Pauline theological assertions include: equal creation in God's image, equal redemption in Christ, mutual submission, ministry as service, the oneness of the body, the priesthood of all believers, the gifts of the Spirit poured out equally on women and men, and equality between men and women in Christ[1] (Gen 1:26–30; Matt 20:25–28; Luke 22:25–27; Rom 1:1; 10:12–13; 12:6–10; 1 Cor 1–2, 7; 9:19; 10:23–30; 11:11; 12:7, 11, 25, 31; 14:1, 26; 16:16; 2 Cor 3:12–18; Gal 1:10; 3:28; 5:1, 13; Eph 2:11–22; 4:2; 5:18–22; Col 3:10, 16–19; 1 Thess 2:7; 1 Tim 4:3; 6:17; Titus 2:4; Jas 2:1–13; 1 John 4:13).

21. Men and women are now one in Christ. Women and men are brought together as equally and completely as Jews and gentiles. All are equally honored in the family of Jesus Christ. All the barriers separating women and men and keeping us from being one body in love and worship are now done away with in Christ. Just as Gal 3:28 has social implications for slaves and gentiles, it also has social implications for women. Gal 3:26–28 is both a theological and sociological declaration. In Jesus, racial, class, and gender divisions are broken down. Women and men are equally valued, equally loved, equally honored, and equally included, and equally able to use their gifts to serve Christ and his body (Gal 3:28).

22. Women and men have the same rights, obligations, conditions, expectations, and honor as each other in marriage. And a man or woman's value isn't dependent on whether he or she marries or does not marry (1 Cor 7).

23. 1 Cor 11:2–16 affirms the differences between women and men, and fully integrates women and their gifts into the body of Christ. There is debate about what *kephalē* ("head") means. But it is clear that Paul affirms women publicly prophesying and praying in the church. This passage does *not* place limitations or qualifications on the public

1. Payne, *Man and Woman, One in Christ*, ch. 3.

ministries that women can exercise, and does *not* teach that women may only serve publicly when they are under male spiritual leadership and authority. Instead, Paul affirms women in ministry in Christ's church (1 Cor 11:2–16).

24. Paul cannot be prohibiting women from teaching and speaking in the public assembly in 1 Cor 14:34–35, because either side of this passage involves Paul encouraging women to speak up and use their gifts. Women and men alike must use their gifts in a way that ensures godliness, orderliness, relational harmony, and credible public witness (1 Cor 14:26–40).

25. Paul describes marriages characterized by mutual submission, mutual love, and mutual self-sacrifice. Paul does ask women and slaves to submit, but he does so in the context of a patriarchy-shaped and slavery-condoning culture. In Ephesians 5 and Colossians 3, Paul describes marriages shaped around *mutual submission*. And he challenges husbands to give up power and control, and to sacrifice themselves and their desires for their wives (Eph 5:21–33; Col 3:11–25).

26. The Bible does *not* prevent women from serving as overseers and deacons. Many English translations incorrectly add masculine pronouns to 1 Tim 3:1–13 and Titus 1:5–9. This gives the false impression that only men can serve as overseers and deacons. Paul charges male deacons/overseers to be faithful to their wives, and female deacons/overseers to be worthy of respect in every way. Paul says anyone can aspire to be an overseer and doesn't qualify this with a reference to gender (1 Tim 3:1). "Whoever aspires" means "*whoever aspires*" (Titus 1:5–9; Titus 2:3–5; 1 Tim 3:1–13).

27. Christians should not build ministry practices and church structures around odd passages that contradict the trajectory of the Bible and the known ministry practices of the biblical author. That is what we do if we use 1 Tim 2:8–15 to prohibit women from certain ministries. 1 Tim 2:8–15 is a difficult passage with some unusual and odd terms (e.g. "women will be saved through childbearing"), and *final certainties are not to be had*. There is evidence that Paul is offering instructions on worship for a specific situation. And we know that Paul did in fact affirm and release women to teach and pioneer and lead throughout the churches. And the trajectory of the Bible is expanding and increasing honor and ministry for women, not contracting and

declining. I conclude that 1 Tim 2:8–15 does not prohibit women from teaching or leadership roles (1 Tim 2:8–15).

28. The Bible doesn't only ask women to submit to their husbands; it also tells husbands to submit to their wives. Mutual submission is the norm in Christ-honoring Christian marriages, as it is in healthy Christian congregations and ministries. Peter and Paul follow the way of Jesus when they tell husbands to relinquish power and, instead, treat women as equals, with honor, dignity, respect, and love (Eph 5:21; 1 Pet 2:13—3:7).

29. The God-given ideal for male-female relationships is love. And Christ showed us that ultimate love is giving oneself away for the other. Ministries and roles come and go. But God is love, and those who live in love live in God, and God in them. In all things, women and men should strive for love and complete unity, so that the world may see that we are one with each other and with God (John 17:20–26; 1 Cor 13; 1 John 4:7–21).

30. The Son is *not* eternally subordinate to the Father, and women are *not* forever subordinate to men. And such theology is out of step with historic Christianity and contemporary Bible-believing evangelical belief. We must be very careful about applying the Trinitarian analogy to human relationships. While I believe that the Trinitarian vision should lead to love, intimacy, mutuality, and communion, I also believe that we must be very cautious—human relationships are not like divine relationships, just as human nature is not like divine nature. We should leave Trinitarian analogies and references out of the discussion about women and men in Christ (Phil 2:5–11).

31. The church must deal courageously with issues of gender, justice, and power. Sexual scandals and abuses of power are too common. We must shape Christian ministry around a shared commitment to shepherding care, service, humility, accountability, mutuality, and love. This will mean confronting systems and institutions that support gender-based domination, patriarchal power, and hierarchical, command-and-control forms of ministry. The Chief Shepherd calls us to a different way (Phil 2; 1 Pet 5:1–11).

32. Christian ministry is about love and service *not* power and hierarchy. Hierarchical and domineering leadership is unbiblical. God calls men and women—together and as equals—to a lifestyle of sacrifice,

humility, service, and love. Together, we reject hierarchy, patriarchy, power, and control. Instead, we seek after Spirit-empowered grace, deep relationships, and genuine humility (Matt 20:20–28).

33. Equality in the body of Christ means there is no place for sexism, racism, ageism, elitism, classism, or any other "ism" that results in the abuse, inferiority, silencing, or colonizing of others. Instead, we seek to live in the way of Jesus Christ together. This means our values are clear and shared and lived out. We reject all forms of sexism and racism. We value humility. Service. Love. Respect. Truth. Grace. Welcome. Embrace. Hospitality. Mutual submission. Honoring the "least of these." This means that as Christian men and women, together, we must choose to reject the desire for power, prestige, and primacy. Instead, we choose humility, service, simplicity, and love, honoring each other and looking out for each other's well-being and interests (Matt 19:30; 20:20–28).

34. In the New Testament, the qualifications for ministry and leadership are spiritual, moral, and ethical. While many of Paul's instructions are directed at male leaders, this does not disqualify women from serving in those roles. As we have seen, English translations at times include male pronouns in the text where none exist, giving a false impression about who can lead. Biblical ministry and leadership qualifications are based on character and the ability to guard the truth of the gospel, and are *not* based on gender. Women and men alike can meet these qualifications, and, therefore, equally serve and lead. "If anyone aspires to be an overseer" means that "anyone can aspire" (1 Tim 3:1).

35. Mission is enhanced and multiplied when women are empowered to serve, pioneer, and lead. Countless generations of pioneering missionary and church-planting Christian women have followed in the footsteps of Junia. Despite restrictions and hurdles, Junia's sisters are leading and expanding the local church and the church worldwide. The church should invest in female pioneers, missionaries, evangelists, church planters, and planters of movements (Rom 16:7).

36. There are countless examples of women and men serving together. Christians should applaud, honor, and learn from women and men who serve as co-apostles, co-leaders, co-pastors, and co-laborers, in church and society. Our credibility and witness and maturity and

diversity are enhanced as women and men serve together as equals (Rom 16:3, 7).

37. Our ultimate vision is that of men and women from every nation, tribe, people, and language gathered before the throne and before the Lamb. On that day, trials and tribulations, enmity and conflict, patriarchy and hierarchy, tensions and misunderstandings, roles and functions, gender domination and institutional abuse, and all forms of pain and sufferings will finally end. This is our shared and ultimate vision and hope. Together, men and women from every time and ethnicity will cry out, together, in a loud voice: "Salvation belongs to our God, who sits on the throne, and to the Lamb. Amen! Praise and glory and wisdom and thanks and honor and power and strength be to our God for ever and ever. Amen!" (Rev 7:9–17).

38. The church must listen and learn from women, and all those who have been historically marginalized and silenced. Together with women, minoritized groups, and other marginalized people, we must seek humble and repentant change. When it comes to women in ministry, our churches and their leaders need to embrace clear, open, measurable, and concrete strategies for empowering and releasing more female leaders. We must act now to amplify the voices and honor the gifts of women. Change requires courageous and practical action. It's not enough to just believe that women should be equal. It's not enough to acknowledge that the Bible talks about biblical equality, mutual submission, and complementarity without hierarchy. We need action for change. We must hear what God is saying to us, and act to change our assumptions, behaviors, and institutions. Be doers of the word (Jas 1:19–27).

39. Christians should honor and tell the stories of male and female historical and contemporary Christian leaders. The church must allow these stories of both female and male leaders to model and inspire discipleship, spiritual passion, the radical and activist life, Christ-centeredness, and perseverance (Heb 11:1–12:3).

40. In conclusion, the biblical picture is one of men and women living and serving together in mutuality and equality in the home and the church. Women can hold any office in the church and perform any ministry. Women, like men, serve and lead on the basis of their gifts and callings, not on their gender. The Bible passages that seem to

restrict women's ministries are very few. And they are not universal prohibitions but, rather, specific instructions for particular situations and contexts. The trajectory of Scripture is expanding gender equality and ministry roles for women. This trajectory is overwhelmingly supported by the biblical evidence. The biblical picture is mutuality and equality in the home and the church. The biblical vision is complementarity without hierarchy, equality and mutual submission in marriage and ministry, and oneness in Christ. We pray for God's grace and power to make it so.

* Note: I do not speak for everyone who calls themselves a Christian egalitarian, or for any church or organization, in this Biblical Egalitarian Manifesto. I only declare what I see affirmed in the Bible.

Further Reading

Here are some books that I've found helpful as I've read about what the Bible teaches on women and ministry. Most of these books or articles come from an evangelical egalitarian position, except for a few exceptions, such as those by Davies, Keller, and Kostenberger.

Bird, Michael F. *Bourgeois Babes, Bossy Wives, and Bobby Haircuts: A Case for Gender Equality in Ministry.* Grand Rapids: Zondervan, 2012.

Cunningham, Loren, David Joel Hamilton, and Janice Rogers. *Why Not Women?: A Biblical Study of Women in Missions, Ministry, and Leadership.* Washington, DC: YWAM, 2006.

Davies, Glenn. "Biblical Study Paper: 1 Timothy 2:8–15." In *Personhood, Sexuality and Christian Ministry,* edited by B. G. Webb. Homebush: Lancer, 1987.

Dickson, John. *Hearing Her Voice: A Biblical Invitation for Women to Preach.* Rev. ed. Grand Rapids: Zondervan, 2014.

Evans, Mary. *Woman in the Bible: An Overview of All the Crucial Passages on Women's Roles.* Milton Keynes: Authentic, 2006.

Fee, Gordon D. *Paul, the Spirit, and the People of God.* Peabody, MA: Hendrickson, 1996.

Giles, Kevin. *The Trinity and Subordinationism: The Doctrine of God and the Contemporary Gender Debate.* Downers Grove, IL: InterVarsity, 2012.

Giles, Kevin. *What the Bible Actually Teaches on Women.* Eugene, OR: Cascade, 2018.

Grenz, Stanley J., and Denise Muir Kjesbo. *Women in the Church: A Biblical Theology of Women in Ministry.* Downers Grove, IL: InterVarsity, 1995.

Johnson, Elizabeth A., ed. *The Strength of Her Witness: Jesus Christ in the Global Voices of Women.* Maryknoll, NY: Orbis, 2016.

Keller, Kathy. *Jesus, Justice, and Gender Roles.* Grand Rapids: Zondervan, 2014.

Kostenberger, Andreas J., and Margaret Elizabeth Kostenberger. *God's Design for Man and Woman: A Biblical-Theological Survey.* Wheaton, IL: Crossway, 2014.

Leach, Tara Beth. *Emboldened: A Vision for Empowering Women in Ministry.* Downers Grove, IL: InterVarsity, 2017.

Lederleitner, Mary T. *Women in God's Mission: Accepting the Invitation to Serve and Lead.* Downers Grove, IL: InterVarsity, 2018.

Mathews, Alice. *Gender Roles and the People of God: Rethinking What We Were Taught About Men and Women in the Church.* Grand Rapids: Zondervan, 2017.

McKnight, Scot. *The Blue Parakeet: Rethinking How You Read the Bible.* Grand Rapids: Zondervan, 2008.

McKnight, Scot. *Junia is Not Alone.* Patheos: Patheos.com, 2011. Kindle.

Murphy, Edwina, and David Starling. *The Gender Conversation: Evangelical Perspectives on Gender, Scripture, and the Christian Life*. Eugene, OR: Wipf & Stock, 2016.

Payne, Philip B. *Man and Woman, One in Christ: An Exegetical and Theological Study of Paul's Letters*. Grand Rapids: Zondervan, 2009.

Peppiatt, Lucy. *The Story of Woman's Freedom: Re-discovering the Mutualist Vision of Scripture*. Downers Grove, IL: InterVarsity, 2019.

Pierce, Ronald W. *Partners in Marriage and Ministry: A Biblical Picture of Gender Equality*. Minneapolis: CBE, 2011.

Pierce, Ronald W., and Rebecca Merrill Groothuis. *Discovering Biblical Equality: Complementarity Without Hierarchy*. Nottingham: SPCK, 2005.

Saxton, Jo. *Influential: Women in Leadership at Church, Work and Beyond*. London: Hodder & Stoughton, 2012.

Sayers, Dorothy L. *Are Women Human?* Grand Rapids: Eerdmans, 1971.

Westfall, Cynthia Long. *Paul and Gender: Reclaiming the Apostle's Vision for Men and Women in Christ*. Ada, MI: Baker, 2016.

Witherington, Ben, III. *Women in the Earliest Churches*. Cambridge: Cambridge University Press, 1988.

Witherington, Ben, III. *Women in the Ministry of Jesus: A Study of Jesus' Attitudes Towards Women and Their Roles as Reflected in His Earthly Life*. Cambridge: Cambridge University Press, 1984.

Links to Online Articles and Resources

I've found these online articles and resources helpful, as well as the websites they are located on. All links are current as of February 11, 2019.

Cervin, Richard S. "On the Significance of Kephalē ("Head"): A Study of the Abuse of One Greek Word." *Priscilla Papers* 30 (2016). https://www.cbeinternational.org/resources/article/priscilla-papers/significance-kephalē-"head".

Giles, Kevin. "Jesus and Women." www.cbe.org.au. https://www.cbe.org.au/index.php/conference-2010/keynote-addresses/jesus-a-women.

Graham, Elizabeth. "12 Ways to Advocate for Women in Ministry." *The Junia Project.* www.juniaproject.com. https://juniaproject.com/advocate-for-women-in-ministry/.

Hill, Graham Joseph. "6 Ways to Empower and Release More Female Leaders." www.theglobalchurchproject.com. https://theglobalchurchproject.com/empower-female-leaders/.

Hill, Graham Joseph. "9 Ways to Amplify the Voices and Honor the Gifts of Women." https://theglobalchurchproject.com/9-ways-amplify-voices-honor-gifts-women/.

McKnight, Scot. "Woman in Ministry." The first in a series of almost forty blog posts by Scot McKnight on women in ministry. The whole series is excellent. https://www.patheos.com/blogs/jesuscreed/2006/09/12/woman-in-ministry.

Mowczko, Margaret. "How Christian Egalitarians Understand Equality." www.margmowczko.com. https://margmowczko.com/christian-egalitarians-understand-equality/.

Mowczko, Margaret. "My Perspective of Christian Egalitarianism." www.margmowczko.com. https://margmowczko.com/christian-egalitarianism-in-a-nutshell/.

Mowczko, Margaret. "1 Timothy 2:12 Archives." www.margmowczko.com. https://margmowczko.com/category/equality-and-gender-issues/1-timothy-212/.

Scholer, David M. "Women in Ministry: A Biblical Basis for Equal Partnership." Fuller Theological Seminary. https://www.fuller.edu/wp-content/uploads/2018/02/Women-in-Ministry-A-Biblical-Basis-for-Equal-Partnership.pdf.

Snodgrass, Klyne. "A Case for the Unrestricted Ministry of Women." http://www.bemidjicovenant.com/filerequest/2991.pdf.

Wallace, Gail. "Defusing the 1 Timothy 2:12 Bomb." *The Junia Project.* www.juniaproject.com. https://juniaproject.com/defusing-1-timothy-212-bomb/.

Wright, N. T. "Women's Service in the Church: The Biblical Basis." www.ntwrightpage.com. http://ntwrightpage.com/2016/07/12/womens-service-in-the-church-the-biblical-basis/.

Recommended Websites

Here are a few websites I highly recommend.

Christians for Biblical Equality (CBE) International
https://www.cbeinternational.org

Christians for Biblical Equality (CBE) International (Australia)
https://www.cbe.org.au

Ezer Rising
http://www.ezerrising.com

Fixing Her Eyes
http://www.fixinghereyes.org

Jesus Creed (Scot McKnight)
https://www.patheos.com/blogs/jesuscreed/

Margaret Mowczko: Exploring the Biblical Theology of Christian Egalitarianism
https://margmowczko.com

The Global Church Project
https://theglobalchurchproject.com

The Junia Project
https://juniaproject.com

Bibliography

Agosto, Efrain. *Servant Leadership: Jesus and Paul.* St. Louis: Chalice, 2005.

Anderson, Robert J., and William A. Adams. *Scaling Leadership: Building Organizational Capability and Capacity to Create Outcomes That Matter Most.* New York: Wiley & Sons, 2019.

Anglican Advisory Council for the Church's Ministry in England. *The Ordination of Women to the Priesthood.* London: Oxford University Press, 1972.

Barth, Markus. *Ephesians.* New York: Doubleday, 1974.

Bevans, Stephen B., et al. "Missiology after Bosch: Reverencing a Classic by Moving Beyond." *International Bulletin of Missionary Research* 29 (2005) 69–72.

Bird, Michael F. *Bourgeois Babes, Bossy Wives, and Bobby Haircuts: A Case for Gender Equality in Ministry.* Fresh Perspectives on Women in Ministry. Grand Rapids: Zondervan, 2012.

Boff, Leonardo. *Trinity and Society.* Maryknoll, NY: Orbis, 1988.

Booth, Catherine. *Female Ministry; or Women's Right to Preach the Gospel.* London: Morgan and Chase, 1870.

Brock, Rita Nakashima, and Rebecca Ann Parker. *Proverbs of Ashes, Violence, Redemptive Suffering, and the Search for What Saves Us.* Boston: Beacon, 2001.

Cervin, Richard S. "On the Significance of Kephalē ("Head"): A Study of the Abuse of One Greek Word." *Priscilla Papers* 30 (2016). https://www.cbeinternational.org/resources/article/priscilla-papers/significance-kephalē-"head".

Cho, Eugene. "Supporting Women in All Levels of Church Leadership." https://eugenecho.com/2011/03/08/supporting-women-in-ministry/.

Davis, John Jefferson. "Incarnation, Trinity, and the Ordination of Women to the Priesthood." *Priscilla Papers* 1 (2010). https://www.cbeinternational.org/resources/article/priscilla-papers/incarnation-trinity-and-ordination-women-priesthood.

Emmert, Ashley. "The State of Female Pastors." https://www.christianitytoday.com/women-leaders/2015/october/state-of-female-pastors.html.

Epp, Eldon J. *Junia: The First Woman Apostle.* Minneapolis: Fortress, 2005.

Finger, Reta Halteman. *Of Widows and Meals: Communal Meals in the Book of Acts.* Grand Rapids: Eerdmans, 2007.

Ford, Lance. *Unleader: Reimagining Leadership . . . And Why We Must.* Kansas City, MO: Beacon Hill, 2012.

Giles, Kevin. "Paul and Women: Was the Apostle a Misogynist?" *CBE International Online Blog* (2019). https://www.cbe.org.au/index.php/articles/conferences/172-paul-and-women-was-the-apostle-a-misogynist.

———. *The Trinity and Subordinationism: The Doctrine of God and the Contemporary Gender Debate*. Downers Grove, IL: InterVarsity, 2002.

———. *What the Bible Actually Teaches on Women*. Eugene, OR: Cascade, 2018.

Graham, Elizabeth. "12 Ways to Advocate for Women in Ministry." In *The Junia Project* (2018). https://juniaproject.com/advocate-for-women-in-ministry/.

Grenz, Stanley J., and Denise Muir Kjesbo. *Women in the Church: A Biblical Theology of Women in Ministry*. Downers Grove, IL: InterVarsity, 1995.

Helland, Roger. "Nothing Leadership: The Locus of Missional Servantship." In *Servantship: Sixteen Servants on the Four Movements of Radical Servantship*, edited by Graham Hill, 32–41. Eugene, OR: Wipf & Stock, 2013.

Hill, Graham Joseph. "An Apology to Victims of Domestic Violence in the Church." In *The Global Church Project*. Sydney: The Global Church Project, 2017. https://theglobalchurchproject.com/apology-victims-domestic-violence-church/.

———. *Globalchurch: Reshaping Our Conversations, Renewing Our Mission, Revitalizing Our Churches*. Downers Grove, IL: InterVarsity, 2016.

———. *Salt, Light, and a City, Second Edition: Ecclesiology for the Global Missional Community: Volume 1, Western Voices*. Eugene, OR: Cascade, 2017.

———. "Women are the Heartbeat of Living Faith." *The Global Church Project*. https://theglobalchurchproject.com/women-heartbeat-living-faith/.

———. "6 Ways to Empower and Release More Female Leaders." The Global Church Project, 2018. https://theglobalchurchproject.com/empower-female-leaders/.

———. "9 Ways to Amplify the Voices and Honor the Gifts of Women." The Global Church Project, 2017. https://theglobalchurchproject.com/9-ways-amplify-voices-honor-gifts-women/.

Institute for Studies in Asian Church and Culture (ISACC). http://isaccnet.weebly.com/about-us.html.

Jackson, Darrell. "For the Son of Man Did Not Come to Lead, But to Be Led: Matthew 20:20–28 and Royal Service." In *Servantship: Sixteen Servants on the Four Movements of Radical Servantship*, edited by Graham Hill, 15–31. Eugene, OR: Wipf & Stock, 2013.

Köstenberger, Andreas J., and Margaret E. Köstenberger. *God's Design for Man and Woman: A Biblical-Theological Survey*. Wheaton, IL: Crossway, 2014.

Kuruvilla, Carol. "Here's Why These Women Don't Want to Live in Donald Trump's America." *Huffington Post* (October 15, 2016). https://www.huffingtonpost.com.au/entry/christian-women-donald-trump_us_580123d6e4b0162c043bdd7d?ec_carp=6686177678725004902.

Lowe, Philippa. "Can Godly Men Be Quiet?" *One Week in August*. https://oneweekinaugust.com/2019/02/15/can-godly-men-be-quiet/.

McKnight, Scot. *The Blue Parakeet: Rethinking How You Read the Bible*. Grand Rapids: Zondervan, 2008.

———. "Woman in Ministry." https://www.patheos.com/blogs/jesuscreed/2006/09/12/woman-in-ministry.

———. "Women in Ministry: Galatians 3:28." https://www.patheos.com/blogs/jesuscreed/2007/04/10/women-in-ministry-galatians-328/.

Mowczko, Margaret. "1 Timothy 2:12 In Context: Artemis of Ephesus and Her Temple." https://margmowczko.com/1-timothy-212-in-context-2/.

———. "1 Timothy 2:12 In Context: The Heresy in the Ephesian Church." https://margmowczko.com/1-timothy-212-in-context-3/.

———. "Women Church Leaders in the New Testament." https://margmowczko.com/new-testament-women-church-leaders/.

Murphy, Edwina, and David Starling, eds. *The Gender Conversation: Evangelical Perspectives on Gender, Scripture, and the Christian Life*. Eugene, OR: Wipf & Stock, 2016.

Payne, Philip Barton. *Man and Woman, One in Christ: An Exegetical and Theological Study of Paul's Letters*. Grand Rapids: Zondervan, 2009.

Petersen, Elizabeth, and Jannie Swart. "Via the Broken Ones: Towards a Phenomenological Theology of Ecclesial Leadership in Post-Apartheid South Africa." *Journal of Religious Leadership* 8 (2009) 7–34.

Pew Research Center. "The Gender Gap in Religion around the World." *Pew Research Center* (2016). http://www.pewforum.org/2016/03/22/the-gender-gap-in-religion-around-the-world/.

———. "Women Relatively Rare in Top Positions of Religious Leadership." *Pew Research Center* (2016). http://www.pewresearch.org/fact-tank/2016/03/02/women-relatively-rare-in-top-positions-of-religious-leadership/.

Pierce, Ronald W. *Partners in Marriage and Ministry: A Biblical Picture of Gender Equality*. Minneapolis: Christians for Biblical Equality, 2011.

Pierce, Ronald W., et al., eds. *Discovering Biblical Equality: Complementarity without Hierarchy*. 2nd ed. Downers Grove, IL: InterVarsity, 2005.

Sandberg, Sheryl. "Why We Have Too Few Women Leaders." https://www.ted.com/talks/sheryl_sandberg_why_we_have_too_few_women_leaders/up-next#t-135387.

Sayers, Dorothy L. *Are Women Human?* Grand Rapids: Eerdmans, 1971.

Schussler Fiorenza, Elisabeth. *But She Said: Feminist Practices of Biblical Interpretation*. Boston: Beacon, 1992.

Snodgrass, Klyne. "A Case for the Unrestricted Ministry of Women." 2008. http://www.bemidjicovenant.com/filerequest/2991.pdf.

Thomas, Christine M. "At Home in the City of Artemis: Religion in Ephesus in the Literary Imagination of the Roman Period." In *Ephesus: Metropolis of Asia*, edited by Helmut Koester, 81–117. Valley Forge: Trinity Press International, 1995.

Westfall, Cynthia Long. *Paul and Gender: Reclaiming the Apostle's Vision for Men and Women in Christ*. Grand Rapids: Baker Academic, 2016.

Witherington, Ben, III. *The Indelible Image: The Theological and Ethical Thought World of the New Testament*. Downers Grove, IL: InterVarsity, 2009.

Wright, N. T. "Women's Service in the Church: The Biblical Basis." Paper presented at the symposium "Men, Women and the Church" at St. John's College, Durham, 2004. http://ntwrightpage.com/2016/07/12/womens-service-in-the-church-the-biblical-basis/.

Zenger, Jack, and Joseph Folkman. "Are Women Better Leaders Than Men?" *Harvard Business Review* (2012). https://hbr.org/2012/03/a-study-in-leadership-women-do.